To my parents on their
Golden Wedding Anniversary
10 August 1970

Critical Affairs

CRITICAL AFFAIRS

A Composer's Journal

NED ROREM

GEORGE BRAZILLER

New York

ALSO BY NED ROREM:

The Paris Diary of Ned Rorem
Music From Inside Out
The New York Diary
Music and People

Acknowledgments

Various sections of this book have previously appeared, sometimes in altered versions and with different titles, as follows:

"Poetry of Music" was originally presented as a lecture entitled "Words Without Song," delivered in April, 1969, at New York University, commemorating the 150th anniversary of Walt Whitman's birth. It was first printed in *London Magazine* and, in abbreviated form, in *The American Pen*. (The lecture was followed with a recital of settings of Whitman's poetry by a variety of composers, sung by Adele Addison.)

"Décors of Sound," when it appeared in the April, 1969, issue of *House Beautiful*, carried the subheading "Musical Thoughts on Emotion and Environment."

Vogue, which commissioned both "The Avant-Garde as Démodé" and "Ladies' Music," published them under the titles "Can't Eat Politics, Can't Eat Art" and "Women: Artist or Artistesse."

"Against Rock" was published in *The New York Times*, October 26, 1969, under the title "Oh, Richard Goldstein, Don't You Groove for Me."

"The More Things Change" is from *Mademoiselle*.

"Sun" was a note for the program of The New York Philharmonic, where it appeared in conjunction with the world première of that piece in July, 1967.

High Fidelity published the obituary on Julius Katchen, and *Harper's Magazine*, the article "Critics Criticized."

Certain fragments from the two journals have appeared in *Cavalier, Avant Garde, Harper's Bazaar, The American Record Guide*, John Cage's *Notations, The American Scholar*, and *The New York Times*.

"Around Satie's Socrate" was a spoken preface to a performance of *Socrate* by Hugues Cuenod and myself on February 10, 1969.

Contents

1

Journal One

IT'S a bad time for music. As the public grows larger, standards lower, and simplistic action precedes intelligent reaction. Disciplined artists are regarded askance, when regarded at all, by revolutionary and right winger alike. The nuance and shape of music, its elegance and depth, are replaced by propagandistic sensuality, even brute force, unrelated to what for centuries the art presumably represented for all. That many sensitive and cultivated people also sanction the trends, suggests that either they've been brainwashed through an understandable wish to stay young, or that (as Charles Ives used to say) I have my ears on wrong.

But those ears are my only compass, and they indicate that the major musical domains of today—from rock to aleatoric to serial to rock—are hopelessly misdirected in a loose, sociological commerciality. Why, my ears ask, do I bother any more, especially when successful practitioners explain that the misdirected looseness and sociological commerciality are the very beauty of it all?

I bother because I'm a composer. Were I a layman, or even a professional Music Lover, the situation could be ignored by restricting myself to sounds I like. As a composer I sometimes feel that my *type* of music cannot defend itself, since it's not for sale like pop, nor deep and dull like. . . . So I momentarily put aside the music quill, take to the typewriter, defensively like other critics, and write about these things.

One distinction cannot be overemphasized: I am a composer who also writes, not a writer who also composes.

*

If a composer could state in words what being a composer means, he would no longer need to be a composer.

I can't write music and write about music during the same period; the two acts stimulate mutually repellent juices.

*

Is art found in the street, in human contact, in the sound of unrehearsed weeping? Such a notion finds buyers because it peddles two unrelated products for the price of one. The promotion rolls out a philosophy, cuts off the dangling edges, and boxes it as art. Or boxes the art as philosophy. The promoters mean their metaphors literally: all the world's a stage, and what's on a stage is of course Theatre. Now, to state there is music in the wind does not prove there is music in the wind.

Twenty years ago there was room for only masterpieces, for only masterpieces had the right to require
the intellectual (as opposed to sensual) concentration
and investigation needed for that period's "in" music.
Yet hundreds then composed *in the genius style*, first
inventing the rules—the justification—then making
their artifacts. Today they don't even invent rules.

*

"What," people always ask, "is music's future?" Are
they asking: what will the future of music be? or,
what will future music be? Either way, like planned
obsolescence in automobiles, the concern is more for
the future than for the present. The nervousness of the
question reveals a very twentieth-century obsession:
the evaluation of art beyond the immediate purpose it
serves, a process that would have been unknown to, say,
Bach. The question—usually posed by the academic
middle-aged—also implies that art, as a "value," is in
a precarious situation, that it *should* last, but probably
won't. Meanwhile, certain young people maintain that
the lasting ingredient makes no difference. As long
as twenty years ago painters were already painting in
"momentary" materials: some of the pictures destroyed
in the Museum of Modern Art conflagration would
have, in any case, disintegrated by now.
The only difference between evaluation now and
twenty years ago is that youth is listened to for its
own sake: the experienced heed the inexperienced.
Music still qualifies, more than ever, both with our
intelligentsia and with our youth (who are by defini-

tion not the intelligentsia) on one of two grounds: either it is so immediate it must be good, or it is so circumlocuted it must be good. The simplicity of the Rolling Stones' message exemplifies the first criterion, the complication of Milton Babbitt exemplifies the second. In neither case does the music's expressive content (what used to be called beauty) seem a prerequisite. Qualifications are: total craftsmanship, or total lack of craftsmanship.

To assert that the past, the classics, are irrelevant to today's life style is to confess a poverty of life, a laziness of style, an irrelevance of the life style itself, and an ignorance of art's inherent intent. Art has never been relevant in a political—an *actionary*—sense. Let's expand the life style to include classics, since art's function, like nature's, lies precisely in its irrelevance to anything but itself.

The concern with the future, or with current life style, supposes that the modern as concept remains vital. In fact, the concept is exhausted. Music's future, as in the past, lies in classifying and disseminating the present, and that future automatically takes care of itself.

*

Because we enjoy Ravel more than Debussy we assume he's less good than. In another generation it will be acknowledged that Ravel is better precisely because he is more enjoyable.

*

Whenever I switch on the radio in the middle of some nineteenth-century but otherwise unidentifiable bombast, it turns out to be Berlioz. I simply can't remember that man's music. Why has it no content for me? Perhaps that's a temperamental question. God knows I'll forgive a French musician anything providing he remains French, lean, and clean. Berlioz sounds German. Yet I dote on German fiction and philosophy, while French fiction and philosophy, especially as exemplified in the *Nouveau Roman* and *Tel Quel*, is exasperation pure. It's only non-French music that's beyond me. Then what of Chopin, whose every measure thrills? Why, Chopin is French, as are Liszt, Delius, Copland, most of the Russians.

*

I do what comes easy: it either works or not. I have found that what comes hard (like the *Flute Trio*, the "solderings" of *Miss Julie* to make her theatrical, book reviews, or articles on musical ideas as opposed to aphorisms) is often less good, too ornate. This paragraph, for instance, would have been better if I'd stopped after the first sentence.

*

I seldom enter a dentist's chair without having to request that Muzak be shut off. Yesterday I arrived for the first in a series of seven expensively tiresome root-canal treatments at the office of oral surgeon Dr. Schwartz. No sooner was my mouth stuffed with rubber clamps and drugging needles than, without my permission, Dr. Schwartz turned on the radio. I gurgled a request that he suppress the sound, which he promptly did. He drilled, mulling for a minute of uncomfortable silence, then said, "That's the most unusual suggestion I've ever had." I gurgled that I was a musician. Pause of disbelief. Then: "Well, if you're a musician I'd think you'd especially like the music." I gurgled that I'd explain later. Another pause. "My son's looking for a good store to buy a case for his guitar. I suppose Mandel's is the best place, wouldn't you say?" Silence.

I never did *explain later*. The point is, no composer can stand being captive audience to any music, especially to a background of undifferentiated mush. He cannot *not* listen. Constantly having his own notes in mind, he doesn't want their perilous ordering disturbed by the insult of piped-in noise at airports, supermarkets, taxicabs, elevators, turkish baths, or dentist chairs. They say Jane Austen worked best with sound surrounding her.

*

If art is both theft and choice, we assume without facetiousness that the great choose wisely whom they burgle. Choice is all. They can even choose to reveal their victims, but that is a cover-up for deeper influences ignored.

From the horse's mouth, so to speak, I speak, and with those mandatory aristocratic rights which have nonetheless afforded no sense of *noblesse oblige* toward other spokesmen. Robert Craft has squatter's rights on public property. He's used those rights well and writes well, perhaps changed history. Yet after all the convolutions have been put in order (who said what and how and in which tongue), it will have been only Stravinsky who lent Craft's words authority.

*

If poetry is criminality or sainthood gone astray, as in the case of Genet, it is also childhood regained, as in the case of——Genet.

Since conservative poets feel the same as far out poets about their poems (wanting words, if not meanings, understood), but since experimental poets are seldom drawn to conservative poets (though Babbitt did use Hollander, and Berio did use Cummings), yet since audiences have a hard enough time just *getting* the words to anything sung by a "concert artist," one concludes that all music dealing with words must necessarily, to communicate in the strictest verbal sense, be simple.

Of course in grand opera words have always been more or less dispensed with—long before McLuhan's literary incomprehensibility of deafening rock—and the music becomes more than human speech can say. Still, this is not babble, nor tribal, but ecstasy organized by one man.

*

Just as illegible handwriting means semiconscious bad manners, so slovenly musical calligraphy signifies a disordered composer. I learned more in six months as a professional copyist than during four years at the conservatory.

*

In May, 1968, I was invited to compose a short opera, with piano accompaniment, for the Metropolitan Opera Studio. The stipulations were two: that the work be "simple enough," practically and intellectually, to present on a tour of schools where opera had never been seen; that there be mutual agreement on a libretto, hopefully an original one.

My first thought for a book was poet Kenneth Koch. I brought him to the Met's assistant manager, John Gutman. They were predestined to misunderstand each other's basic English. Still, Kenneth was inspired to write three and a half librettos in two weeks, all rejected by Gutman and his staff. Kenneth was nonetheless paid (out of my advance), and I was left to contend with a situation I swore would never recur. There followed a long series of letters, "ideas exchanged," between Gutman and me and Mark Schubart, the vice-president of Lincoln Center's education committee which was putting up the money. We never reached an understanding. I went ahead anyway and composed an opera on Kenneth Koch's already famous play, *Bertha*, and submitted it to Gutman. It was refused, as was another small opera I felt impelled to write simultaneously (on Gertrude Stein's *Three Sisters Who Are Not Sisters*).

Recently, under the title *The Birth of Bertha*, I organized the correspondence into a sequence resembling

Laclos' *Les Liaisons dangereuses*, whose characters hang themselves without their author's editorializing. What follows is my last letter on the matter, which, when received by Gutman, caused him to reply: "If you allow me to be rude for once: there is at this point no other opera [but the Metropolitan]."

5 March 69

Dear John—

I appreciate the tactful frankness of your letter; it permits a similar candor from me. I agree that we disagree. We probably always will: the reasons seem fundamental. Thus I've not sent the score of *Bertha* nor the Stein play to Mark Schubart, since I don't see that his opinion could finally alter anything. Perhaps, though, you'll lend him your copies.

I'm glad to note that you will release *Bertha* for inspection elsewhere, because clearly we should call a halt to our enterprise which has already cost both anxiety and money. But I'm glad, too, that you hold no hard feelings, that you continue to profess admiration for my music, and that perhaps the studio could present a reading next season.

While shaking your hand, I feel obliged to say that you are making a mistake. The Met Opera Studio, theoretically so valuable, shows signs of inheriting the atrophied blood of its parent organization which, like mad Queen Bertha herself, forever pursues the same old objectives. I would not question your rejection of my little opera if your response were to its quality rather than to its genre; yet your claim that it is too "sophisticated" bemuses me. Sophistication no longer means anything since the advent of Camp and of McLuhanesque mass media wherein any art can be enjoyed by anyone on any level—rather like Elizabethan theater. Nor could *sophistication*'s former usage (intimations of rarefied and snobbish irony) ever have applied to *Bertha*'s open hilarity. Indeed, the very lack of sophistication combined with an innate awareness in young audiences—*all* audiences—today, allows them to accept and reject instinctively, without intellectualizing.

By this token, your reaction to Gertrude Stein as unviable contradicts fact. In recent years her plays have proved not only culturally but commercially successful. Forgetting that Thomson's two Stein operas are frequently and joyously performed by undergraduates, or that Kupferman's *In a Garden* is a college staple, what about Al Carmines? Carmines, a composer who writes music not unlike mine (though less "sophisticated"), set Stein's *In Circles*, performed it in Judson Church for over two years for capacity audiences consisting of every possible milieu, age, and sex. Gertrude's scenario, though written years before the Thornton Wilder one-acter which we considered, remains vitally original, while the Wilder has grown simplistic and (in the worst sense) old-fashioned— something kids would laugh at, not with. If these kids are unsophisticated, i.e., inexperienced, then *The Barber of Seville* should prove as uneasy-going as *Wozzeck*. Why not let *them* judge?

God knows I'm not an artist trying to be with it. But neither am I out of it. My literary judgments surely have much to do with whatever may be my professional status as a composer; as such I am interested in contributing to the field of opera on my terms. It is doubtful if the Opera Studio's board members will find a musician who, in accordance with their terms, would produce other than a rehash.

*

To *Time* magazine, who wanted "something quotable" for a cover story on a rock group called The Band:

29 November 1969

Having listened carefully to The Band I can't really share your reactions.

A few songs linger agreeably. *In a Station*, for instance, was attractive with its mildly unexpected contours of tune. Or *Weight*, with its unaffectedly clean harmonies. *Whispering Pines* pleasantly recalled the cooing of the Hi-Lows a dozen years ago, while *I Shall Be Released* was a reminder that a good melody (Dylan's) stays good no matter who sings it—though the words are awfully corny. Also I rather liked *Chest Fever*, maybe because it suggested my own music, or at least one of my musical devices (the constant reiteration, *à la* Satie, of a four-note motive). But they could have done so much more with it!

Indeed, that was my feeling with most of The Band's work. The aftereffect is one of undifferentiation: the tunes are neither distinguished in themselves, nor distinguishable from each other: I can't remember them, and I have a good memory. Elsewhere there is not enough color or invention to make up for this.

The "why" is uncertain. Perhaps it's their very lack of pretension (which in rock means lack of insolence) that winds up sounding pretentious. Unpretentiousness as a *raison d'être* becomes meaningless unless replaced by something else—by charm, or fantasy, or whatever.

Such blandness may be due to their Canadian origins. Like Switzerland in relation to France, or Holland to Germany, Canada has always seemed a boring reflection of England. The boys in The Band lack the Stones' perversity or the Beatles' whimsy. Sure, they're healthy and horny, but these qualities aren't necessarily necessary to art. I hesitate making the comparison, but they demand it:

they are the same, but *not as good as*. In aiming low they hit their mark. But they lack the magic touch.

As a musician I naturally focus on the music here, an element ironically neglected by critics ("intellectual" and otherwise) of rock. Your emphasis too, at least in your memo, is on their "message," which I don't take seriously. The Band's *sound*, especially the vocal excruciation of *Unfaithful Servant* and *Lonesome Suzy* would be risible if it weren't so phonily sincere. Why must professionality be viewed suspiciously by the pop world? Barbra Streisand may not "mean" more than The Band, but she sings on pitch, which means plenty to a cultivated ear.

The Band, in my opinion, is not worth a coverage in the section of *Time* presumably devoted to musical events, much less a cover story. On this, I can only repeat what I said on the phone: *Time*'s recent evasion of important music areas (important, at least, to me) reads like managerial proselytizing for pop, not like reportage on a special part of international culture. The Sunday *Times*, keeping its musical pages intact, has created a new section for pop which is, after all, more a sociological than an artistic phenomenon. Follow suit.

Personally I find that whole scene degenerating, and have lost interest in what is no longer interesting. You are forcing The Band. How many geniuses can we expect per decade, anyway!

*

The verse of our national anthem was superimposed by Francis Scott Key onto an old drinking song—which is perhaps why everyone sounds drunk when intoning it. Yet even to the truly drunk it scarcely inspires nostalgia, as does *Dixie*, say, or *La Marseillaise*. The unmusical masses are more quickly converted than one might suspect to "new" music, doubtless because they *are* unmusical. Why don't we find a composer who, with a decent poet, might write a new song for America? Because the need no longer exists as an inherent sentiment?

The Star Spangled Banner is a narrow and vicious piece: bad poetry on bad music expressing bad sentiments. And its performance grows increasingly bad as our sense of whatever patriotism is broadens, along with our musical sophistication.

If, like Hamlet's soliloquy, our anthem's every clause has become a family bromide, the verse isn't for that any "good." Nor does it extol, as other countries do, the beauties and virtues of our land, but the virtue and beauty of war, as though war were a fireworks display. It's not for nothing that *We Shall Overcome* has displaced our national anthem in the hearts of many thoughtful young today.

*

A recent issue of *Music & Artists* contains a round-table talk between Morton Gould, Otto Luening, and Ned Rorem on the subject of music's future. It also contains an interview with Thomas Schippers who, at the interview's end, is told by the interviewer that their exchange will appear in the same issue as the Gould-Luening-Rorem round table about where music is going, and what does he think of *that*. "I don't know what to think," answers Tommy. "One thing I'm sure of: Ned Rorem doesn't know where *he's* going."

No, I don't know where I'm going. Does anyone? Does Stravinsky or Ava Gardner or de Gaulle? But I know the direction I'm heading: forward. Schippers heads backward. As a conductor of mostly Romantic repertory he lacks the legitimate authority of a Lukas Foss to presume as to my direction. Were Foss to question my direction I'd worry, for whatever he may think of it, Foss does perform my music. Schippers doesn't. Nor does Schippers perform any music that is "going" places. He maintains that his remark is not intended as an insult, but I take it as one.

*

Some writers make pictures not badly: William Blake, Henry Miller. When they turn to composition the result is less horrendous than banal: Gerard Manley Hopkins, Paul Goodman. Is there an author who has had musical composition as a hobby and gotten away with it?

A certain kind of author, adored by his homeland, remains inaccessible to other nations. That monuments like Racine or Pushkin are unappreciated in translation is understandable; poetry has always been a fragile traveler. That novelists like Hawthorne, Svevo, or Alain Fournier don't cross their frontiers is as mysterious as the collective unconscious.

Another kind of author, adored by his milieu, remains inaccessible to other sensibilities. That sacred bulls like Hamsun or Hemingway are devoured by every tongue is understandable: earthiness has no boundary. That writers like Pavese, Cavafy, or Djuna Barnes are restricted to a cult is as bizarre as the fame of their inferiors who owe them all.

14

So it is with music, which is far from a universal language. But a musical composition's international viability is precisely opposed to its literary equivalent (if there is such a thing!—it's fun to play games). The music of Racine, Pushkin, Hawthorne, Svevo, Fournier, would be Lully, Tchaikovsky, Billings, Respighi, Debussy, whom most people love. That of Hamsun and Hemingway would be Grieg and Antheil, whom nobody loves. And for Pavese, Cavafy, and Barnes we have Malipiero, Hadjidakis, and Griffes, beloved of us all.

*

Art exists mostly in the body. The torso thinks. Which is why we react differently at noon than at midnight. Intelligence is a chain reaction. The wolf-child, the gazelle-boy, never got chained, and so were illiterate.

*

People born in the same country at other times and places speak separate languages. But although over-forty is very different from over-thirty, we all remain pretty much forever as we were at four. A painter's style may change beyond recognition, but not his signature.

To be young is no accomplishment. To be young in heart is abject. Young and New aren't synonymous. The only people as dumb as the young are the old (not forgetting the middle-aged). To be aware in heart is an accomplishment.

*

The futility of originality. Is new music new? And Oscar Wilde wore a sunflower, bigger than the Maharishi's. Who's cultured today? The same aristocratic percentage as in Attic Greece and Elizabeth's England. Who cares about them? Not I, for one, why I won't even bite their hand anymore! I've given up meat. But we have to eat *something!* To object that tomatoes scream as we devour them is to lend humanity rather than vegetality to their nervous system, if they have one. Surely, if we wish to study tomatoes' reactions to our biting them, it will not be through their vocal cords.

*

Well, I could vomit, thinking of all I've discarded over the decades before knowing that even scraps would be good, years later, for Income Tax. When a piece was copied, inked, and orchestrated, the manuscript was confided to the incinerator. Once published, the ink copy got burned. And all those letters thrown out! Gentle or fiery words from the now dead—thrown out. Love notes—thrown out! Glamorous receipts thrown out or, at best, defaced and pasted into scrapbooks. Mislaid forever are ones from (I blush) John Alden Carpenter, Madge Evans, Margaret Truman.

*

Olden patronage was practical, commissions fulfilled necessary luxuries, served a purpose. Like Jackie Gleason today, music then was to cruise down the river by (Handel), go to sleep by (Bach), feel a little night by (Mozart), and above all to get married and buried by. Music was functional, the opposite of cultural.

Is culture killing art? If the Medicis encouraged art-for-a-purpose, Fromm now encourages experimentation for experimentation rather than for his own pleasure or pain. And outside of the university, out there in the streets, since there is everywhere drama, why bother to call it drama? But isn't drama more correctly what is not accessible to all?

*

History concerns the present. Klimt's Judith has not just emerged from Holoferne's tent, not even via King James' version, but from a bedroom in Freud's Vienna. *The Sign of the Cross* depicts Hollywood in 1933. *Henry the Eighth* is about Charles Laughton. The first Globe Theatre productions didn't pretend to be costume dramas; Cleopatra dressed like Elizabeth.

Music too is *so much* about he who performs it! Would Schumann recognize his *Etudes* as (gorgeously) played by Ashkenazy? My own music of ten years ago concerns my reactions to the world of ten years ago, caught there like a grape in Jello. (Fact: Paderewski's heart is lodged in the vault of a Brooklyn bank, floating in formaldehyde like a grape in Jello, maintained by Poles protecting their anti-communist reputation.)

Pasolini's taste in music (Marian Anderson in *Saint Matthew's Passion*) is as intrusively naïve and wrong as Maurice Jarre *(Doctor Zhivago)* is intrusively slick and wrong. Each mistakes history for the past, and for his *own* past.

*

The preponderance of Bouleziana dazzles by means of intelligence. But what music does Boulez *like?*—for one needn't assume he necessarily likes what he conducts. . . . He is more American than I because he equates validity (if not quality) with progress. But innovation for its own sake is just that.

For art, we are offered equations and logic and things unrelated to art which nobody enjoys but is afraid to admit it. Art, though perhaps sprung of suffering, has always been enjoyable suffering. An artist may represent his period without resorting to his period's mechanisms, since merely to inhabit a period is to represent it.

Experience is naturally the source of anyone's material. But there is confusion between writing *from* experience and writing *of* experience—between building on, or only reliving.

*

Talk of the weather is not, as custom has it, an evasion of less superficial matters, but the profoundest subject of human exchange. Weather tints our mood, enters every room of our life-span like ectoplasm dictating the tone of all existence.

*

Pointillism is another painting term often misapplied to music, especially to music of the classical twelve-tone composers because of their way of notating isolated pings. Pointillism is not an esthetic but a technique opposite to Webern's. A painter amasses separate points so that from a certain distance they blur into a solid. Thus the harmonies of Debussy, perhaps of Strauss or even Bach, are more truly "pointillist" than those of Webern, whose pings are never condensed.

*

The promotion of his own work, by means professional and social, is as necessary for the composer as the orchestration of that work. This has probably always been so. Certain composers—Carl Ruggles, for instance, or Lou Harrison or Paul Bowles—who disdain the practice and live recluded, nonetheless arrange for understudies. Recording and rehearsing for performance of one's own music, although less "artistic," are much more time-consuming than the actual composing. I now lose interest even before the first presentation, and would rather my time be occupied in unrelated activities.

When obliged to hear my own music in the company of others, I'm prisoner of their boredom.

*

"The serious composers of each generation, whether Beethoven or Schoenberg, are always, with few exceptions, accused of over-intellectuality." So speaks Goddard Lieberson, former chief at Columbia Records. He is wrong.

Serious composers are by nature exceptions, so who are the exceptions to these exceptions that are *not* accused of intellectuality in each generation? Was Palestrina or Handel or Mozart or Chopin so accused? Is *accuse* the word? If Beethoven was "accused," he was also widely worshiped. Who, in the generation of Schubert, Liszt, Brahms, Tchaikovsky, Wagner, were the overly intellectual and who the exceptions? In which category falls Ives, or Ravel, or Bartók? Granted, Hindemith in the 1930's was called cerebral; for that has he gained Olympus?

Why not more correctly label them all Misunderstood?, since understanding (assuming art is ever understood rather than felt) changes daily, and since an *œuvre réussie* supposes too many layers for total absorption simultaneously by an artist's public, his peers, or even by himself. Artists anyway care less about being misunderstood than about just being heard. To be misunderstood is hardly an exceptional complaint: we are all misunderstood most of the time.

Being over-intellectual is pretty much a twentieth-century concept, though the supposedly serious music of Honegger, Sibelius, Britten, Prokofiev, indeed of most of Stravinsky, never suffered the appellation. For Schoenberg the appellation *was* true, in that for him the delicate balance between talent and technique (formerly termed heart and head) overweighed toward the latter. Nowadays, to be accused of cerebrality, is for a composer to have arranged his publicity well. Yet people no longer care about the publicity, much less

about the music publicized which they never hear anyway. They would rather read about a musician's
whimsy than his depth.

Now Lieberson's successor at Columbia, John
McClure, states with naïve dismay that "the world of
serious music has tended to be parochial and to fright-
en off rock-oriented kids." Could it be that these kids
are less frightened than disinterested? that they don't
take serious music seriously anymore because, after
years of starvation, they have found a digestible antidote?

*

Since the above was noted, eight months ago, it seems
that the Columbia staff has itself grown "rock-oriented," sporting long hair and compulsory beards.
Serial music is out, electronic music in (but strictly as
an offshoot of psychedelia, like Hermann Hesse or
Scriabin), while rock is *the* big promotion. And the
promotion is dictated by accountants. Big classical
names no longer sell, neither on disc nor on the road.

*

In *My Sister Eileen* a poor and starving Roz Russell
ponders the label of a cornflakes box: Tastes Delicious
with Strawberries. "What doesn't!" she exclaims.

Rock freaks are always telling you: it sounds divine
under pot. Though surely they know that music is not
inherently altered by circumstance any more than cornflakes are by strawberries. Who cares—except for

claims that rock is rendered art through its persuasion to the masses? Even these claims would bother me less were I a Music Lover rather than a composer. There *is* a difference.

Pot has always been identified with music more than with other arts because it affects time. Time slowed down gives time for perception, explains why the uninitiated can distinguish between several simultaneous counterpoints, and why performers grow capable of unprecedented intricacies, although the endlessly unvaried rhythms of Moroccan orchestras also thrill us, as Gene Krupa used to, with ceremony. But marijuana cannot change the ceremony into art any more than incense can change the motion of high mass into ballet. More important: if drugs render the hitherto tone-deaf into musicians, albeit undiscerning ones, they also render musicians into critics. Now most critics know that most music is bad, and if they are also composers this holds for their own music. The Acid Test is for an artist to judge his own work under acid. This will not make him a better artist. It will show him where he has cheated.

*

Since freedom in art—if not in art's promotion—has been achieved, what's to be done with it? Since we can all do our own thing, what's the thing? The concept of masterpiece as a master's piece has been discarded as a pietistic anachronism. Just as the best restaurants have the least pretentious décors, the best Berio or Beatles' ballads hold up when stripped of their trappings, or when compared with their rivals who come and go. And they are professional: professional in quality like Stravinsky, not just in commerce like the Rolling Stones.

Music, like freedom, has become a business, every last aspect of all of it. The business of pleasure. To defend any expression on other grounds than professional quality now is dreary. Professionalism will have to be the premise for future artistic utterance, unless the utterance be shouted down with the millenium along with so many other standards.

2

Poetry of Music

With a Postscript Honoring Whitman

IF the arts inherently expressed or even resembled each other, we wouldn't need but one. Still, oftener than they are differentiated they are likened. The most frequent comparison is of music with architecture though these are the farthest apart.

Music serves no purpose beyond itself, and the identifying property of that self is motion. Architecture does serve a purpose beyond itself, and its identifying property is static. Architecture would thus seem closer to painting or sculpture, while music—as flow—obviously resembles dance, or even prose. Yet unlike prose, or even dance, music has no innate content, no symbolic sense. If a building has symbolic sense, the primary function is nonetheless practical. An architect cannot improvise, thinking up a plan and the plan's execution as he goes along the way artists can. An architect who omits a beam will see his structure collapse, if he overlooks a bathroom the tenants collapse. When an artist fails, no one but himself really gets hurt; his work is not useful.

Music then inhabits an opposite pole from architecture, with prose and painting falling somewhere between.

*

Since music lacks content beyond itself, can it then be compared with poetry? "What does it *mean?*" people ask of a poem. About music they do not ask *why*—at least not in the sense of its dealing a double standard, of being beauty that instructs. When singers question me on the significance of the words to a song, I answer: They signify whatever the music tells you they signify. What more do I know about poetry?

Poems are not Why. They are Because. Comprised of both question and answer they mirror music more singularly than any other human enterprise. Perhaps because of their common quality, poetry and music often marry. Now the marriages, however seemingly ideal to outsiders, are all based on misunderstanding at best, at worst on total perversion.

Having his verse set to music is not necessarily the ultimate compliment a poet may receive from a composer. Yet many poets today covet the idea, at least before the fact. They ponder Beethoven and Schiller, Schumann and Heine, Ravel and Mallarmé, those sublime collaborative unions wherein the poets' words were illuminated while presumably remaining the same —the same, only more so! Actually those unions were not collaborations at all. They were settings of a *fait accompli*, the *fait* being verse able to stand alone, the *accompli* being a denial of that ability, resulting not in

25

"the poem only more so" but in a transformation: a song. The song often bemused the poet who, though maybe pleased (more likely dismayed), never quite recognized his original impulse. After all, had he not heard his own "music" while composing the poem? Naturally no musician hears that poem the same way, or why would he write a song?

Song is the reincarnation of a poem which was destroyed in order to live again in music. The composer, no matter how respectful, must treat poetry as a skeleton on which to bestow flesh, breaking a few bones in the process. He does not render a poem more *musical* (poetry isn't music, it's poetry); he weds it to sound, creating a third entity of different and sometimes greater magnitude than either parent. It too may ultimately stand alone, as those nineteenth-century songs now do despite being disowned at birth by their poetic fathers. *We* hear them as totalities without considering their growing pains.

Indeed, much past poetry is known to us exclusively through song settings, hence our unconscious assumption of such poetry's emanations of musical inevitability. Yet when it comes to his own work, today's poet has his own notion of inevitability. He is torn between a need to hear his words sung, yet for those words to retain their initial beat and echo, their identity proper. His "proper" must obligatorily be sacrificed; his notion of inevitability becomes the fly in the ointment. The only inevitable way to set poetry is the "right" way, and there is no one right way.

Song is the sole example of one preexisting art medium being juxtaposed intact upon another. The words of the poem are not *adapted*, like film scenarios from plays; they remain unaltered while being tampered with, and unlike other musical forms—fugue, for instance, or sonata—there exist no fixed rules for song.

There are as many "right" ways for tampering with a poem as there are poems and good composers, or different viewpoints of a single composer toward the same poem. A composer's viewpoint is right if it works, regardless of the poet's reaction. For the poet will never feel the song as he felt the poem which inspired the song. Debussy, Fauré, and Hahn all used the same verse of Verlaine, all convincingly, all more or less differently. More or less. *Clair de Lune* did suggest a similar built-in musical formula to French composers at the turn of the century.

On the principle that there is no one way to musicalize a poem I once composed a cycle by selecting eight works by as many Americans and setting each one to music twice, as contrastingly as possible. The performing sequence of the sixteen songs was pyramidal: one through eight, then back from eight to one. Although each poem is repeated, none of the music is; thus the poems supposedly take on new impact at second hearing not only by virtue of being sung at a later time, but also by being reinvested with another shape.

*

It goes without saying that I speak here of poetry as distinct from lyrics. Poetry is self-contained, while lyrics are made to be sung and don't necessarily lead a life of their own. The best lyricists are collaborative

27

craftsmen. When "real" poets write with song in mind they fail both as poets and as lyricists because, in "helping" the composer, they overindulge in presumably felicitous vocables which emerge as self-conscious banality. To argue that they *hear* what they write is irrelevant to musicians; we have come a long way since Homer, and poems today are mostly made and absorbed in silence. A poet declaiming his own verse is no more definitive, no more *inevitable*, than some composer's setting of that verse. This applies as much to readings of always-the-same verse against never-the-same jazz backgrounds as it does to the embarrassing solo histrionics of a Dylan Thomas or the sabotagingly dry delivery of an Elizabeth Bishop.

*

Elizabeth Bishop in Brazil and I in France corresponded for years on such matters. Finally in 1957 I made a setting of her masterpiece, *Visits to St Elizabeths*, recorded it with a mezzo-soprano, and sent the disc to Rio where it was awaited with high expectations. The tact of Elizabeth's disappointment was touching. "I wonder why you picked a female voice," she wrote in 1964, "and how it would sound with a male voice." Again, in 1968: "Sometime I'd like to write you one small critcism—not the music, of course, but the manner of singing it." Finally in 1969: "My complaint is that it sounds too hysterical. I hadn't imagined it that way, somehow. Yes, I had thought of a male voice, I suppose—but I don't believe that is what bothers me. It is the fast tempo and the increasing note of hysteria. Because the poem is observation, really, rather than participation . . . something like that. Two friends have said rather the same thing to me. It is awfully well sung, nevertheless. I don't know whether it could just be *slowed* down, or not? Probably not." (Cruelly I'm reminded of Saroyan's poignant remark to Paul Bowles about the latter's music for *My Heart's In The Highlands*. "Couldn't it be played more—well—in *minor?*")

Poets' work ends with their poems. During the concert they can only weep impotent from the wings, especially when the song succeeds. *Visits to St Elizabeths* in fact succeeds more than many of my pieces, being often sung, loudly applauded, and singers say it "feels good." How answer Miss Bishop when the song imposes its own terms of longevity?

As to the singer's sex she has a point, but a point of taste, not quality. In principle, we cannot distinguish blindfolded between male and female pianists, say, or violinists. A composer hence has a stricter concept of piano and violin attributes than of the human voice. He is more lenient of *varieties* of interpretation given one song by many singers, since a soprano is by definition more limber than a baritone. Nothing precludes a woman's persuasively singing a man's song at a faster speed if within the speed she maintains a logical attitude. (The reverse is less convincing, at least in opera, not for musical but for esthetic reasons. While we can empathize and even weep with Octavian or Cherubino, a man in a woman's role is only good for a laugh.) As for a man performing the Bishop work, I like the idea, though the reality would sound top-heavy, it being a patter song.

*

Once I judged a contest for young composers. My duty was to select the best from some two hundred manuscripts. An unconscionable percentage were settings of *The Hollow Men*, all for male chorus, and all starting with the first-thing-that-comes-to-mind solution: open parallel fifths. Which may explain why T. S. Eliot never granted musical rights to anyone.

*

Not that Howard Moss disapproved of my musicalization of his long *King Midas* suite, though certainly his sonorous concept (a concept after the fact) was not like mine. The songs are lean and western, while he saw (saw, not heard) eastern opulence. Yet for the final publication his only request was sizable billing, he being more concerned with rightful recognition than with sabotage. After all, the poetry hasn't been stolen: it's still right there in his book.

Poets' names are seldom seen on song covers, and usually omitted from printed song programs. Yet where would the song be without them? Where, though, would the singer be without the song whose composer is given proportionately short shrift? And returning full circle, where is the poet without the singer? "But I am not without the singer," answers the poet. "The singer is myself, and what you call illuminations are to me evasions."

*

Good poetry won't always lend itself to music, i.e.,

won't of itself make good music even if the composer is good. Some poems more than others cry out to be sung (their authors' wishes, like Eliot's, notwithstanding), though different cries are heeded by different composers with different viewpoints on dealing with those cries—whether to clarify, dominate, obscure, or ride on them.

Still, better good poetry than bad. Music, being more immediately powerful, does tend to invisibilize all poems except bad ones. Despite popular notions to the contrary, it is a demonstrable fallacy that second-rate poems make the best songs.

Theodore Chanler may well have become America's greatest composer of the genre had not his small catalogue adhered to mainly one poetaster (Father Feeney) whose words sound even sillier framed by lovely tunes which, through some inverted irony, end up being subdued by those words. Duparc gained Parnassus on a lifetime output of only thirteen songs; yet I wonder how they'd come off with other verse than Baudelaire's. Chanler just may make it on his eight delicious *Epitaphs* based on the solid words of Walter de la Mare.

*

Despite whatever reputation I may hold in this area, I am not *just* a song composer in the sense that Duparc was. My three hundred plus songs written since childhood add up to as many hours labor and as many minutes hearing, nothing compared to the long labors of symphonic orchestrations and other works in the larger forms. Yet inasmuch as all real music is essentially a vocal utterance, be it *Danny Boy* or *Petruchka*, I *am* just a song composer.

If less is more, one great song is worth ten merely adroit symphonies. To say you can have it for a song, is to sell the form cheap.

The form, of course, is whatever the composer feels the verse dictates. (The verse, so to speak, dictates its own execution order.) Until the age of twenty-three my songs were built largely upon the dictates of "singable" poetry from Sappho through Shakespeare to Hopkins. Then for a decade in Europe I composed in whatever language I thought I was thinking in. (Incidentally, my songs in French seldom get done, nor do any French songs by Americans. If a French singer condescends to sing an American song, he—or rather, she: it's invariably a she—will go all out and learn one in English, for better or worse. And when an American singer decides to learn a French song, she finds it more *legitimate* to learn one by a Frenchman. Britten has set, in the author's tongue, poems of Hölderlin, Rimbaud, even Pushkin, but they are sung mostly by Britten's ever faithful Peter Pears. Nor am I aware that Italians, for instance, are given to performing Britten's marvelous Michelangelo sonnets. Of course, Italians only sing arias anyway.)

During those first twenty years of song writing, I also used regularly the sounds I most normally inhale: American poetry, especially that of friends, some of whom made words expressly for my setting. Words, not lyrics.

Take for instance Paul Goodman, who was once my Manhattan Goethe: the poet to whom I as a balladeer most often returned. From 1946 his verse, prose, and theatre beautifully served my short tunes, choruses, and opera. Lives shift, ever faster. We seldom meet anymore, in either speech or song. Paul today seems more drawn toward guiding the political thoughts of the young; this can't be done through poetry. And I grow more withdrawn. Yet lately while rehearsing his songs all written in France during the early fifties (a period of Weep and the world weeps with you) I became rekindled with a need for the words and music of that easier decade. The rekindling has not fired more songs of the sort, but it has cast light again on a bit of conversation between old friends.

Or take Frank O'Hara, whose young and recent death placed both a shroud and halo over that vital group called the New York School of Poets. The last of several occasions for which we conjointly conceived an idea was a Poulenc memorial. Alice Esty invited this collaboration. Frank made a poem I couldn't understand and didn't want to set. So he made another which I couldn't understand but wanted to set, and did. As a musician I "understand" poetry not during but only after the fact of setting.

Nor do poets *understand* music, thank God. So-called radical poets, like O'Hara and Goodman, usually in their musical taste are conservative. How often one finds sprinkled through their pages the names of Beethoven, Saint-Saëns, Rachmaninoff.

Take also the poet John Ashbery who writes his *Glazunoviana* while editing *Art News* which is, by definition, about the new (as over in Paris the up-to-date Françoise Sagan drops the name of Brahms!). Ashbery supplied the words to my vocal trio, *Some Trees*.

The words were no problem, for the music does not make them a problem: I didn't try to illustrate their sense, but to underline their sound. Poets want their words (if not their meanings) comprehended. The farther out the poet, the nearer in must be his musician.

*

I compose what I need to hear because nobody else is doing it. Yet I feel guilty about what I do best—setting words to music. Because it comes easily, meaning naturally, I feel I'm cheating.

*

My songs are love letters. To whom? Like Vladimir Nabokov, I write "for myself in multiplicate," meaning for friends, those personal extremities. Are unheard melodies sweeter? Intelligence is silence, truth being invisible. But music does not (should not) appeal only to our intelligence, nor is it especially concerned with truth any more than poetry is.

Yet we're all afraid of being misrepresented, as though we didn't misrepresent ourselves every minute. A song is but a single facet of ourself, which the listener takes as the whole self.

*

In the foregoing do I contradict myself? Very well then, taking good Walt Whitman's prerogative, I contradict myself. Not that, like him, I am large or contain multitudes; but he taught me not to fear contradictions. The purest demonstration of fearlessness is nudity, whose purest demonstration is song, whose purest demonstration is the poet's eternal Myself.

"I pour the stuff to make sons," he exclaimed. Those sons cover the earth, singing for better or worse through the impulse of their father. More than anyone in history save Shakespeare, Whitman has appealed to song composers whatever their style or nationality, possibly because he spoke as much through his voice as through his pen, contagiously craving immortality. "I spring from the pages into your arms," cries the dead author to his living reader.

The act of reading is no more passive than being a spectator at the theatre, despite what sponsors of total-audience-participation would today have us think. To read is to act, it takes two to make a poem, an attentive reader participates constantly. But with Whitman the participation becomes more than usually evident, more physical. The reason may lie in his emphasis on immediate sensation rather than on philosophic introspection. At least that explains his century-old appeal to musicians, and his more recent revival within our collective poetic sensibility, specifically with Allen Ginsberg, and generally with the flower children of Pop culture. That explains also why so many primarily instrumental composers, when they do write an occasional song, set the poems of Whitman to music. (Or set their music to the poems of Whitman!) Finally it explains why so many of us primarily vocal composers started early with Whitman, especially during the 1940's when it seemed urgent to be American at any price, and why so many of these songs sing embarrassingly now like the youthful indiscretions they are. During that same period but for other reasons (reasons of gratitude), certain riper Europeans used Whitman, and used him more touchingly than many of us—Kurt Weill, for example, or Hindemith whose *When Lilacs Last In The Dooryard Bloomed* is surely his choral masterwork.

My own choices of words have usually been somehow more practical. When planning to write a song I seek poems more for sound than meaning, more for shape than sentiment. Sometimes (this is a confession), the music being already within me, I'll take literally any verse at hand and force it into the preconceived melodic mold. When the outcome "works," it's precisely because I have not wallowed in the sense of the words so much as tried to objectify or illustrate them.

But Whitman has proved exceptional to this kind of choice. For if I loved form for its own sake and challenge, I also loved and needed Whitman whose style, in a sense, is lack of style: an unprecedented freedom which, with its built-in void of formal versified variety, offers unlimited potential for formal musical variety. Whitman is content. A poet's content is a musician's form; any other way a song is merely redundant and becomes, in the words of Valéry, like a painting seen through a stained-glass window. Looking back, I find that the dozen Whitman poems I have musicalized over the years were selected less from intellectual motives than because they spoke to my condition at a certain time. I adopted them through that dangerous impulse called inspiration, not for their music but for their meaning.

The first was *Reconciliation*, an appeal to my pacifism in time of war. A few years later *Sometimes With One I Love* so sharply described my frame of mind that the music served as a sort of superfluous necessity. But once, when commissioned to provide accompaniments for recitations of Whitman, I of course failed; for if the human voice in song is the most satisfying of all instruments—indeed, the instrument all others would emulate—the spoken voice is the least musical, and a sonic background to it simply interferes.

Another time, however, I was so overcome by the sensuality of *The Dalliance of the Eagles* that song was not enough. In a tone poem called *Eagles* for huge orchestra I composed a purely instrumental tissue on Whitman's strophic format, and followed (symbolically, if you will) his development of idea. Listeners, aware of the program, are appropriately titillated by the sound picture of æreal carnality, though of course no nonvocal music really connotes an unvariable picture beyond what the composer tells you, in words, it's supposed to connote.

Contrary in resources, if not in intent, were my 1957 settings of five Whitman poems for baritone and clavichord. And in 1966 I turned to this catholic writer for help in still another domain. I was plotting a large-scale suite for voice and orchestra titled *Sun*, and I proposed to use descriptions of that star by eight poets—from King Ikhnaton in 1360 B.C. to the late Theodore Roethke. At a loss for a penultimate selection (I required something tranquil, almost motionless, before the final explosion) I turned to Whitman as naturally as some turn to the Bible and found, not to my surprise, in his *Specimen Days* a prose paragraph to answer my prayer, whose low key proved the high point of the cycle.

*

Much current enthusiasm for Whitman, indeed for any admired artist, centers less in quality per se than in how that quality applies to our times. We hear a good deal about protest and involvement, with implicit hints that a committed artist is a good artist—or vice versa. The premise is false, for talent is conspicuously rarer than integrity. An artist speaking politics succeeds on the strength of his name; he is not speaking art. The prime movers of public thought have never been major artists who, almost by definition, are not in positions of authority; when they are, their art atrophies. Romantic though it sounds, artists need time, time for the introspection of creation. That time cannot be spent in the obligatory extroversion of "committed" oratory. Anyone can be right; nor are artists necessarily invested with rightness. Their function is not to convert so much as to explain pleasurably— albeit with sometimes agonizing pleasure. At least that's how I understand *my* function.

Yet when I consider my musical use of Whitman I can, in a sense, see it as *engaged*. Still, the song *Reconciliation* is not the product of a pacifist but of a composer who happens to be pacifist, just as *Sometimes With One I Love* is not the product of a lover but of a composer who once felt the experience. How easy to misread the intent of these songs because they have words! The misreading may declare them good when, in fact, they could be bad. Actually no non-vocal music can be proved to be political or committed, and by extension neither can vocal music nor any other so-called representational art.

Having heart and head well placed, then, does not inherently produce art, though it's safe to assume that most artists are no fools. Genius bigots like Wagner are really exceptional; artistic natures do tend to the compassionate left.

Thus it was not Whitman's good intentions that made him what he was, but his expression of those intentions. And with mere contradictory words, what more can I say of Whitman's intentions that hopefully I've not said better with music?

3

Against Rock

As social phenomenon rock is ever more intriguing, though as musical experience it is now virtually nil. Writings around the subject thus prove more provoking than the subject itself, being embroidery on bright fancy more than on dull fact. Yet when such writings pose as criticism, even as sociology, they usually fail. They fail because they concentrate on the "layers" of meaning in the sappy poesy rather than on the basic music, or because when concentrating on the basic they do not judge or even appraise, but describe mere sensual experience. Not that such experience is only "mere," but it *is* rather undifferentiated, sensuality being anyone's property.

These critical matters are growing more critical. For example, the Rolling Stones' *Sympathy for the Devil* has lately received the same psychoanalysis that the Beatles' *A Day in the Life* got three years ago. Whereas *A Day in the Life* will remain a landmark in the literature of great song, *Sympathy for the Devil* is terrible music with terrible words, terribly performed. To poets or musicians worthy of the name, that contention would seem too self-evident for further elaboration. For them this chapter ends here.

The music fails at the age-old device of imposing its matter through insistence rather than nuance, that is, through literal repetition rather than development. As with all unsophisticated techniques, only high quality can sustain it, which explains the staying power of monotone Moroccan chants, Kentucky mountain tunes, Ravel's *Boléro*, the Beatles' *Hey Jude*. When quality is low, the effect is like that of a child's tantrum drowning error in noise, which explains why so much pop (so much anything) evaporates without residue. True ease is hard; the gift to be simple is not freely offered to just anyone. The Stones are fake simple, without gift. Their *Devil*'s design lacks arch, the sonic element is without sensibility, much less invention, and the primary harmonies are not simple but simplistic. Neither does the melody flow anywhere, nor does its stasis invite hypnotism rather than boredom.

Misfired simplicity, then, makes this music bad.

The words too pretend. Since Now becomes instantly Then, their timeliness is feigned, while timelessness remains beyond their control. Mick Jagger's presumably-guilt-inspiring whine of "Who killed the Kennedys?" is cheap Brecht, just as Jim Morrison's apparently gasp-making declaration "Father I want to kill you, mother I want to ----" is pseudo-Freud. So what else is new?

How many outrages are today indulged in the name of relevance! That a man is concerned with justice—is engaged, as the saying goes—doesn't make him an artist, since art may be truth, but truth alone is not art. *Guernica* is great not because it's political but because it's Picasso. Billie Holiday didn't need "meaningful" lyrics to grab your heart; her one Strange Fruit came from a basket of familiar corn, much of it rotten but which, on her Midas tongue, turned gold. Her repertory was of nonprotest staples by, at best, Kern and Gershwin. I suspect but can't prove (nor can you disprove) that what we now detect as her Black resentment was actually the tone of private love affairs turned sour. Her words weren't bad because they weren't "good": they didn't aim to be With It on every level.

What makes Jagger's lyrics bad is their commercial up-to-date before-the-fact intent.

The vocal performance is doubly false, for the diction and timbre emulate the Negroidistic accents of Bob Dylan, himself an ersatz Billie. Imitation is no sin: even the most innovative art is inherited; through rejection we still seek our parents—but we *choose* the parents we seek. Yet for artists, choice grows more selective than for Cordon Bleu cooks. Primary rule: pick prudently those from whom you steal.

His inability to revamp plagiarism into personal style because of superficial (even dishonest: he's a white Englishman) instinct for choice, makes Jagger's performance bad.

Terrible music performed terribly: hardly a rarity, after all. Yet if I do not cite fifty other cases, that's because indignation is matched only by overratedness, overratedness growing more out of hand than the very artists themselves like, say Albert Schweitzer or Barbra

Streisand (though the latter has proved rather more professional than the former), characters simply not up to their overblown image. My resentment only flowers in inverse proportion to misplaced adulation.

To balance the record there exists, of course, terrible music beautifully performed: Miss Holiday proved this with a hundred songs, as do many concert pianists now digging up nineteenth-century camp, supposedly to counteract the coldness of "our times." As for beautiful music beautifully performed, this seems so rare that we each possess our small treasure of examples, while beautiful music badly performed seems so common as to require no examples at all.

*

If most rock is such terrible music, why its popularity not only with the great unwashed but with every level of journalism? Is it because most of us, not being "poets and musicians worthy of the name," settle for the mediocre? Or more likely, because rock is not heard essentially *as music?* Quality has certainly never been a prerequisite for popularity, though publicity has, and today publicity concerns itself strictly with the crest of the wave which soaks literally everyone. Some who put down Louis Armstrong (try with closed eyes to distinguish him from Jagger!) enjoy the Stones because they're Now, a criterion identical to the mid-thirties left-wing right-for-the-wrong-reason veneration of Shostakovich and John Jacob Niles. Folk song and Soviet symphonies are almost invariably liked for extra-musical reasons, for what liking them *means.* But since rock doesn't mean anything as either high poetry or persuasive politics, can we like it for the music? As the musical value is low, we must hope its medicinal impact lies in its stimulation of mass camaraderie, a stimulation that comes more from the mere fact of rock's existence than from the sound. Woodstock's 1969 Rock Festival is a case in question: most of the kids didn't even hear the music. But they proved other points of value. Which is fine, but not art.

The conclusion that finally we have Art For The People (indeed, Great Art, since it speaks to all) insults both art and "the people." The conclusion presumes art must be denuded of subtlety, must spell out the obvious for common needs. Anyway, what people? The bathetic stanzas of Mary Baker Eddy, promoted and functioning precisely like rock, are as effectively persuasive to another large group. But does that group's maintaining such verse is art make it art?

Pop critics are spokesmen of, rather than reporters for, the people. They tell me my preconceptions prevent my grooving with the Stones—"You've got to *feel* that sound"—as though feeling were not a question in Debussy and Bach as well. This is hardly reliable commentary, much less criticism, nor is it relevant. Who cares how pop critics groove? If the New Criticism's visceral, anyone's a critic: we all groove more or less the same. What are these scribblers that we should prefer their physical reactions (just a reconfirmation of our own) to their perceptions of a piece of music? Must they take literally Ortega's motto, Against Interpretation? What are they that we regard their hallucinations more than our own, though theirs and ours are provoked by the same circumstance?

They are, of course, the Richard Goldsteins of this

world, illegitimate offshoots of the already dubious Music Appreciation Racket. In stating that a critic's function isn't to "tell us what's good or bad anymore," Goldstein renounces responsible standards, substituting hyper-personal bodily impressions; why should he claim to "know," art now being so ephemeral? Why, then, bother to notate his impressions, even to collect them in a book, *Goldstein's Greatest Hits*, captured for posterity, a posterity which will hardly be Now? The new critics' prose, the Goldstein syndrome, stems from the unrevised stream-of-consciousness inspirations most frequently submitted in Freshman composition. It is a kind of rambling poetry which, since its subject matter also is poetry (the fact of rock is nothing if not poetic), defeats its own purpose, like defining a word by using that word or depicting disorder in an undisciplined style—chaos cannot symbolize chaos. Such vagaries represent to professional criticism what most rock represents to the musical world: calculated improvisation, self-promotional and indiscriminate. Of course it sells. Like rock.

*

Rock sells to a gigantic audience. Clarity therefore is no more required of its defenders than it is of Hollywood advertisers. One message nonetheless shines through: coexistence is taboo—coexistence with the musical past or with other exponents of the musical present. This intolerance (read ignorance) of non-rock music corresponds to the so-called avant-garde composers' intolerance of so-called traditionalists. A contradictory attitude, since rock freaks nominally are of compassionate natures. When they admit to being fed up sometimes with much current discography and wonder where to turn, does it never occur to them to hear *L'Enfant et les Sortilèges?* Do they know what it is? Is relevance only today? When is today? Can they be turned on just by rhythm, not by tune? Do they know *Le Sacre du Printemps,* or even who composed it? *Sacre* does have heavenly tunes, and one can hardly say it lacks a beat. But it *is* twice-thirty years old.

Their patronizing of their elders is not hip, but old as youth itself, and about as intelligent as anti-Semitism. To "think young" implies, paradoxically, that one is no longer young.

Criticism as pure enthusiasm, with its resulting incoherence, its art-is-whatever-I-say-it-is obsession, ironically resembles the stance of the forementioned avant-gardists. Inasmuch as the works of Stockhausen or Babbitt are not kinetic or sensuous, their literary defenses are not musical so much as philosophical. Grooving is not involved: one doesn't *enjoy* their music any more than one "enjoys" Kant or Aquinas. So the explicative prose of a brainy Pierre Boulez or of a brainwashed Joan Peyser deals less in mind-splitting trips than in mindful logic. In extreme forms, as in the quarterly *Perspectives of New Music,* such prose can be as funny as its opposite number in the *Village Voice.* Or in a sheet like the new *Contemporary News Letter* where one reviewer confesses his inability to "say more" because lack of a score precluded analytic notation.

*

Certain high circles claim criticism as *the* literary form today. Still, no matter how constructive, criticism is not self-nourishing like the Novel or the Sonata, but a predominantly parasitic category (which includes, of course, the present essay). The category contains highs, Auden and Sontag, Thomson and Stravinsky, all creative artists speaking from the horse's mouth. The category contains lows, and the best example of the worst that's happening in the new visceral criticism is Richard Goldstein, because he imparts no appropriate information: he does not illuminate the music, but offers only his reaction to the music. His is the tone for them all, though none so brash as Goldstein in his transparent longing to at once chastise and be embraced by the establishment.

The new critic has become a built-in part of rock itself. Seeing the scene from inside out, he lacks a legitimate reviewer's objective vantage point.

If rock is really a polemical environment, like Woodstock, it can't be reviewed as music, since music's function is not to persuade by stating social truths. Yet if rock does present itself as music, preempting the location of classics in the culture of the young, it needs literate defense. Such defense is nowhere forthcoming. So the young swallow the falseness of rock's promotion as unquestioningly as others swallow Madison Avenue which is no more expensive and false. The pity is that the promoters, in concentrating on rock as the sole art of today, no longer bother to resent all other art, because for them no other even exists.

4

Julius Katchen

1926-1969

THOUGH possibly no less beloved of the gods than Mozart or Schubert who died young, successful executant musicians—at least nowadays—are mostly governed by healthy longevity as though renown itself (plus the adrenergic drive that seems coupled with renown) nourished their survival. When a great virtuoso dies after a long life of outward appreciation and inner fulfillment, our sadness contains a reassuring calm, as when the curtain falls on a perfect play. But when a youthful performer is stricken at his height we again see Orpheus murdered by those who are jealous of his song. The irony of such a fate today is often its artificiality. Young Ginette Neveu, for instance, or William Kapell, were among the first of the sky-traveling generation to gamble (and lose) at crowding as many concerts into as many parts of the globe as possible. Theirs was a twentieth-century death.

For Julius Katchen none of these generalities holds. Throughout his life his dazzling talent inspired enough adulation—and his intensity of concentration enough energy—to endure for centuries. He gambled (and won) at the international game: he was world famous through annual personal appearances. Yet he died young, not violently, nor even like a performer so much as like those composers of the romantic era he most adored. Not since the similar passing of Lipatti in 1950 has the piano world suffered such a loss. Theirs was a nineteenth-century death.

Precisely because of early fame and jet-orientation, today's crop of pianists maintain they have no time to learn new works; nor do many of them feel impelled to, at the fees they get for playing old ones. By contrast Julius Katchen commanded at any given time some fifteen recitals and three dozen concertos performable on a few hours' notice. This command was due in part, of course, to a loving curiosity about all music (no one is too busy for what really interests him). It was due also to a bizarre endowment. His lightning-quick learning and his notoriously faithful memory of what he learned came not from intellectual retention but from what might be termed eidetic fingertips: his hands had total recall. I remember first hearing him play all five Beethoven concertos on one program. I remember him memorizing the *Diabelli Variations* from scratch in three days, and my own *Piano Concerto* in less. I remember him going on tour without his music, not because (like the *incroyable* Yvonne Loriod) it was all photographed in the brain: it was photographed in his hands.

What I remember began twenty summers ago when we met, through Gérard Souzay, on the terrace of a Saint-Germain café. Like his pianism, Julius' social style was not cerebral but emotional, that is, direct and very friendly. We immediately grew as close as a composer and pianist can grow, in that I wrote music specifically for him to play. I tailored my tunes, not (consciously) around my abstract interior, but around what I knew he could do, which fortunately—in a sense —was anything. Through him, rather than through the average, did I learn.

Paris, which was then my new residence, had been Julius' home since shortly after the war, and was to remain so until the end; he even came to be known as a French pianist. The reason for his choice of domicile was more social than musical. For one thing— and this was his personal tragedy as well as America's —he never was a prophet in his homeland once he left, although Europe considered him one of the greatest United States exports and elected him the first pianist to make an LP record (Rachmaninoff's *Second Concerto*). For another, his exceedingly American character was attracted by the urbane exoticism, his palette by the high cuisine, and his Judaic-Quaker training by the sensual freedom, of France. The language he spoke perfectly, multilinguality being one of his major talents, a talent, incidentally, mistakenly thought to accompany musicality. He ultimately bought a most Parisian house, married a bright French girl, and had a very French son.

Nonetheless, I cannot remember his ever playing Debussy or Ravel or, in fact, any French music. His musical heart lay generally in Germany, particularly in Brahms. The French, never known by catholicity of taste for culture beyond their frontiers, found Brahms, at least in the forties, as novel as Americans then found Ives. In his final years Julius played Brahms almost exclusively, everywhere presenting the complete solo piano works of that composer in a series of four recitals. Once he confided that while performing the *F-minor Sonata* his involvement was so total that he felt he was fertilizing the universe.

Exclusivity of taste, however, excluded only French classics. There exist few major American or Russian piano works that did not appear on his programs, and his encouragement of young composers in Greece, Turkey, and Spain was not merely verbal. He played them.

To assume that his freak gift for quick mastery was a casual process is to ignore that our gifts in the long run are paid for, and sometimes the price is terrifying. Julius Katchen worked very hard. His vitality was such that after some twelve hours of practice he could go out and make the rounds of bars with the rest of us, get up early next day and start again. Repose was not his obsession, not if it precluded knowing all sorts of people and cultivating fans. For me this boundless interest and force, this unifying of day with night, indicated that, like Baudelaire, he lived three lives in one. Which means that when he died last May he was not forty-two years old, but one hundred and twenty-six.

5

Décors of Sound

Room after room,
I hunt the house through
We inhabit together.
Heart, fear nothing . . .
    —BROWNING

Rooms. They contain our lives. Wards, cradles, nurseries, parlors, boudoir and bathtub, kitchen and sacristy, even the halls of open fields bordered by leafy wall and blue-gold ceiling. Even the coffin. Throughout life and death we cannot escape our rooms. We are the fingers within their glove, corridors of either velvet or iron: the hand inside moves according.

*

According to our environment we choose our environment—our glove, our room. As hands we react tactily But as persons attached to those hands we react with heart and mind, and with the five senses which interact with mind and heart and sometimes with themselves, especially in artists who say they can see sound, sniff green, hear marble, taste terror, and fondle F-major. Still, the arts are specialized and are all, without exception, either visual or auditory. Yet they have been said to derive from that most painful of pleasures which is nostalgia.

Paradoxically, nostalgia arises through those two senses with which no art primarily deals: taste and smell. They can't be channeled, intellectualized, communicated, as can sight and sound and sometimes touch. Tongue and nose single-mindedly burrow through diamond-hard culture barriers to instinct.

*

After a decade's absence I returned to Morocco. Even before reaching Customs the indigenous odors of tea, mint, dung, olives, cedar, unleavened bread, newly tanned cowhides, and burning wet leaves (here in Rabat—like those in my Chicago childhood!) assailed dormant responses well before I'd seen or heard a thing. The pain of this pleasure now is in recalling the pleasure of that pain then: it is nostalgia, otherwise called emotion. I could transcribe such emotion into notes here today in this room far from Morocco, and those silent notes would form a composition to be translated into sound years hence at some concert hall far from this room.

*

Every room has its own music. It is we who put the music there. Morocco was one of my rooms, a haunted room reached by an inexorable path of choice leading from the playpens of a midwestern kindergarten where we sang nursery rhymes, through an adolescent bedroom where I first played the records of Debussy and Benny Goodman whose sounds transformed the drab rug into a quivering carpet which flew me finally across an ocean. On that later return Morocco became (though places never are!) even better than before. Before, though, I was of an age to provoke situations —as who doesn't?—wherein I could play both criminal and victim. Today I justify and protect myself, and so miss out. But I choose what I miss out on.

If I'm no longer anxious to gather sacks of rosebuds while I may, it's not that the flowers might wither, leaving me holding the bag. I'm just no longer interested in rosebuds.

(While typing that last word this occurred to me: wasn't Rosebud the name on Orson Welles' sled, that symbol of lost youth toward which at the film's end the camera pans slowly through a giant room strewn with crates containing every object around which had been built the emotional empire of Citizen Kane?)

*

It's another way of saying that music, like love, must be selective.

But do not confuse love and music. Outsiders say that steady love would provide inspiration for the composer. Inspiration (which no artist thinks much about: if he didn't *assume* it he wouldn't be an artist) is not "provided" but emerges from solitude, while love, as outsiders surely realize, comes from outside. Love furnishes the soul as mirrors furnish the house. Furnishing keeps one out of mischief, but is otherwise unnecessary. Of course music isn't necessary either, although, like mirrors, it does reflect and shows us who we are.

*

If musical art has always reflected what we call "the times" without proposing solutions to the times' problems (solutions must be sought elsewhere), it has also rendered the times—tedious or terrifying though they may be—through what is generally conceded to be communicative beauty. Music cannot not be beautiful, even when ugly.

*

The impact of a musical composition depends on where it's intended to be performed, and on our bodily state when we hear it. Obviously a good frame of mind is required for the attention of "right" listening. So is a good frame of sight. To listen well we must be in familiar surroundings so that visual novelty will not distract us into merely hearing. Hearing can let music go in one ear and out the other, while listening lets music go in both ears and stay. A virtue of the musicale in former times was its encouragement of hearing.

The musicale never thrived in our practical land. Even in France, after a long red- (I mean blue-) blooded activity, the salon has died of anemia. The final transfusions were offered by a beautiful widow, the Comtesse Jean de Polignac, née Marie-Blanche Lanvin and nominal head of the *maison de couture*. Twelve regulars gathered weekly in her dining room where, beneath a fresco created by Bérard to suit the countess' coloring, they would consume breasts of guinea hen, pure gold lemon soufflés, and champagne from the Polignac vineyards. They then adjourned to a grand upstairs parlor where more guests would arrive, and there followed three hours of musicalizing:

sometimes Auric and Février rambling through Chabrier at the two huge Pleyels, sometimes Poulenc accompanying his own nasal wail in the première of a recent cycle, perhaps Marie-Blanche herself informally singing Monteverdi with her friend Nadia Boulanger, or more formal recitals by eminent soloists or composers who happened to be passing through Paris— Menuhin, maybe, or Copland. Thus were all Sundays until Madame de Polignac's death in 1958, Sundays of dedication among friends, of music in the home.

But such a home! My first visit there rendered me tone-deaf. The wall of that upstairs parlor happened to be covered with Vuillards, the floor with velours, the twenty-foot couches with satin, the ashtrays with pearl, the air with Arpège, and the hostess with a never-the-same Lanvin creation of apple-green chiffon or fairy-tale organdy, all this garnished (between "numbers") with that theatrically succinct résumé of which French is made, be it Sartre's or Suzy Solidor's.

Is this any way to hear music? Yes, once the grave young United States composer that I was had grown accustomed to luxury as "tone" rather than as vice.

*

The rich American living room is remarkable for functional spic-&-spanness, for expensive necessities, the owners feeling a bit guilty about beauty for its own sake (their Matisse is for investment more than joy); wealthy European counterparts, though the ceiling may need drastic repairs, will glow with be-rubied *objets d'art* serving no other purpose than to be looked at. My first evening *chez* Marie-Blanche I *heard*. Not until my third could I *listen*. One Sunday we repaired for our music to a hall that I had never seen. The hall, permeated by tuberoses, Renoirs, and diamond guests, obliged me, as a listener, to begin from scratch. That evening's mixed media was a preview of our Electric Circus.

Being a subtler mechanism than the eye, the ear is crushed by new environments. From the première of a new ballet, albeit one by Stravinsky and Balanchine, it is sights more than sounds we bring home.

*

When in 1965 a work of mine was played at the White House (how *clean* the rooms were there!), nobody including myself listened to my music: the physical circumstances were too special. Yet we all remember whom we saw. If I was offended by the audience's inattention why not, by the same token, be offended by my own?

"Right" listening? Which is the *right* way? Any way, if it gives pleasure.

Once I expressed indignation on learning that a painter friend worked while his phonograph played masterpieces. The composer in me was outraged—the composer who felt his every note merits an undivided sequence of responses from all hearers, and whose definition of masterpiece was rigid. Yet that painter had a larger whistling acquaintance than I with the overall opera repertory, and he loved, he *needed* music in *his* way. How should I judge, I who orchestrate with the radio on? In any case a good artist—even a bad one—knows how to blank out.

*

A decade ago I felt that music's definition, for the first time ever, wanted enlarging. For the young it had come to fill logical, not emotional, needs. I could not deny, but resented, the evolution because my own musical language remained "expressive"—a dirty word in those days.

Emotion in music is whatever you call it. Better still, whatever reaction music provokes may be called emotion—even though some listeners claim to be "mathematically satisfied." (One wonders, then, what *math* does for them?) Now, the kind of music and the kind of reaction alter with the needs of each generation, although the cause-&-effect relation remains invariable. What Mahler supplied fifty years ago is today easily caricatured when our needs are met by electronics.

*

Are our needs indeed met by electronics? It seems more than coincidence that while the new dizzying fertility of science was being mistranslated by musicians into the overcomplicatedly inactive cerebration of formal concerts which nobody would admit were just plain boring, the Beatles reared their welcome heads.

Music is a symbol, which is just another word for theatre which in turn means a distillation of life. Symbols, distillations, to be communicated take discipline. Much of today's music, in its attempt to symbolize chaos, has itself become chaotic. Disorder cannot effectively represent disorder.

I myself compose simply, less because of, than despite, the complexity around me. I always have, being by nature neither follower nor leader. Yet I never thought of this simplicity as an antidote, though perhaps it has finally come to be that; perhaps a mirror as well, inasmuch as Rock also has reverted to simplicity while representing—more than any other cultural emphasis—the "times."

*

So good old emotion in its subtlest embodiment is returning to music, and the music in turn returns to our parlors on phonograph records. Brought about full cycle, the home is again the scene. But the music is no longer an accompaniment, it is accompanied by flashing baths of sensuality that would have thrilled Scriabin in their happening.

*

The Happening. Supposedly this new art, which by definition happens but once, is meant to alter your notion of yourself—to change you. But what do you use for art after you've changed? The Happening's activity may be, if anything, philosophical or religious, a community worship, group therapy—a plurality. For me art's singular. Change us? The greatest—Bach,

Rembrandt—never made such a claim! Indeed, they never made claims, except perhaps to serve. The wider today's claims the narrower the product. Much current art is merely advertisement: to be moved by it is to *pretend* to be moved.

*

Music's impact upon the senses is less dependent than, say, painting's, upon the visual surroundings—despite the sumptuous discomfort at the Comtesse de Polignac's. Nevertheless, a painting in a museum is not the same as at home. (Nothing's the same when we bring it home, a person or a picture.)

Nor is the fashionable contention valid, that all sound is music and that all ways of hearing are musical, for though this might stimulate the consciousness and render the concert hall nicely arbitrary, it would also render the concert literally endless and drive us all mad. Where's the control here for the harmonious emotional environment, the discipline of art? As a composer I need silence.

*

Reading of Fauré's anguish at oncoming deafness made me wonder how that predicament would affect me. Certainly I'd relinquish music before sight: the enjoyment of music is overbalanced by the torture of sound. Deafness, what's more, might make me a better, a more *considering*, composer: there'd be less facile-lush sounds and more dictates of the inner ear. Though what's wrong with facile-lush sounds? And who can prove the inner ear's more perceptive than the outer?

*

I am not an author who happens to compose, but a composer who happens to write. If this paragraph is never completed but dissolves right now, will anyone (myself included) ever really care? However, if this afternoon I improvise a strand of melody, tomorrow and over the following days that strand may lengthen and continually double back upon itself to weave a slow carpet of music which never never never before existed. These words are anybody's. But the musical carpet, no matter how dreadful the pattern, is mine, and will remain always faithfully on the floor of my private room.

6

The Avant-Garde as Démodé

Artists and intellectuals
must deal with politics
only insofar as it is necessary to put up a de-
fense against politics.
—CHEKHOV

TANTRUMS of the avant-garde no longer need the mass publicity they've earned. The point has been proved, their rights have been granted, their revolution is won—like it or not. Many of them do not like it: their work's over, so their work must begin. Finally free, they still seem caged by bromides, for freedom and art are not synonymous.

The consumer-oppressor has paid the rebels' ransom, receiving little in return beyond amateur admonitions that we are all artists. He finds himself literally with his pants down. How, with current discouragement of analysis, must he take this? By merely reacting, never questioning? If everyone's an artist then no one's an artist.

*

I often betray but never defend my music: it must defend itself. Nor is my responsibility to be knowledgeable or even interested in Where It's At. Artists are allowed intolerance of each other along with the world, as demonstrated both by myself and by the young. My intolerance grows compassionate at seeing youth's pat dismissal of the past: destruction of the traditional is traditional. But my intolerance grows disdainful of contemporaries like Lukas Foss or Julian Beck: iconoclasm is unbecoming to the middle-aged. How can they keep up with every trend and still work with coherence?

*

"What do you think of modern painting?" Gertrude Stein's famous reply, "I like to look at it," did not answer the question. She offered reaction rather than opinion. With her as ally I reply, regarding certain modern music: I hate to hear it.

What modern music? If once the world was balanced between church and state, today sacred and profane are one, as are classical and pop. In most of it the time-honored balance between reflection and antidote is uneven: art as society's mirror shimmers like Narcissus' pool wherein the Music Establishment is drowning without crying help.

That Establishment, so far as "serious" music is concerned, is maintained in our larger universities through foundation funds granted largely by academic colleagues. Musical art and academic concerns are, if not antithetical, no more synonymous than music and freedom, as may be seen in the advancing number of young and not-so-young composers whose need to vent genuine concerns is not counterbalanced by talent.

Intellectual conviction is confused with expression, sound with sense. Commitment does not make music, yet the *fact* of commitment is persuasive enough to cause both paid reviewer and small paying public hesitation before disdaining the evermore predictably disorganized insults flung their way.

Most of these words apply to pop as well, except that pop's public is large. If in university music, emotion has been replaced with protest, students are not protesting these protests. Not that students find such protests irrelevant, they just don't find them—or rather, don't hear them over the thunderous sound of their rock.

To criticize a genre is specious, of course; one must determine only how well a work succeeds within a given genre, on its own terms. But inasmuch as any of this music aims at extramusical goals, it grows useless.

*

Still, as Wilde said, art is useless anyway. You can't eat it. You can't eat politics either. Some music *does* seem to be self-generating as well as beautiful. If kids today don't care about Art with a big A so much as events, it's another way of saying their art is nourishing. Works of art thus paradoxically become ornamental necessities or, like certain women, necessary luxuries.

*

That sentiment smacks of aristocracy. Risking the guillotine, I hold to it. Art has never been just anyone's property while retaining its property as art. The past four years have spawned ever fewer genuine works in any form; this, I feel, is due to the direct alliance of art with the New Left. If the state of body and soul appears better for it, the state of music as a lasting social contribution is worse.

*

Art and politics in America have never until recently been closely related. Not that artists lived in ivory towers, but their involvement was extracurricular. Even during the ironically stimulating Depression, the WPA made only nominal friends of politics and art. Nor did the war engender political American arts, perhaps because it did not physically concern us much. Nevertheless, by cutting us off from the cultural dugs of Europe it did wean us into an autonomous adolescence with new imagination added to old brute force. The imagination cultivated fantasy and reflection, dealing with crisis as nostalgia rather than as immediacy. But the youthful breed of novelist, composer, and playwright spilled forth oceans of now classic masterworks.

The period thrived less than a decade. The young grew up. Their elders labeled them the Apathetic Generation, though in fact the Beatniks were driven with an urgency for natural emancipation. Their decade of the 1950's saw music's decline as a fine art, despite the rise of such distinguished craftsmen as Boulez. Nobody but his colleagues cared much. How could people *enjoy* Boulez' complexities when John Cage's fun was guaranteed culture, as was the simplistic gorgeousness of Elvis Presley who began to be sanctioned by the intelligentsia? The intelligentsia spokesmen had now replaced fiction with criticism. As escape from such critical reading one listened to the rhapsodic chants of Allen Ginsberg against backgrounds of a soon-to-be-outmoded form: jazz.

The Kennedys brought the initial conjoining of art with the political scene. However, government acceptance of artists—mostly famous performers—was less official (read financial) than social, as exemplified by invitations from Jacqueline Kennedy. Elsewhere emerged the Hippies, gentle offspring of the Beatniks —themselves heirs of Bohemia—whose art work, like their play (indeed, the two were one), was communal, thus political. This art was manifest in general by "new" mixed media and in particular by rock groups. Some inaudible signal, some psychedelic flare, caused the five invisible jars that once contained our separate senses to overflow into each other with orderly confusion. Yet the artful mixing of media for purposes of collective ecstasy predates the Catholic mass. The originality of the best rock lay not in its presumed experimentation—what was called its *sound*—but precisely in its spontaneous reversion to simplicity as antidote to the "modern" music of concert halls which people were still afraid to admit they hated. Like most great art, the best rock was amalgamated, and quite unoriginal in style.

Rock's first function was to inspire again the visceral response of song and dance after the apathetic decade of head-in-hands listening to cool jazz or serial cerebrality. Its later function, with Lyndon Johnson's advent, was to speak out, tell it like it is. In this guise it became *the* art of our time, addressing itself to, and being accepted by, every social layer including classical composers trying to keep up. But gone now is the spontaneity. Arrived is a crass self-promotion so successful that it is bought and displayed as soberly by *Time* magazine as by the *East Village Other*.

Like the beaten-to-death Living Theatre, mixed mediators compare their arbitrary results with the calculated formality proceeding from professional creativity. In true revolutionary spirit, they seek to supplant the latter with the former, coexistence being alien to the anarchistic modes which amateurs invariably adopt when moving in. Certain delusions were essential for the elevation of mixed-media happenings to pretentious levels, one being the notion that group therapy can be Art. Another delusion, that mixed media was Revolutionary, therefore new, can be attributed to ignorance. But the grand delusion was that mixed media would, by sheer magnetic charm, destroy the performer-audience format forever.

The first delusion stems from the premise that any self-expression can be Art. This is definition by no definition: it can as easily be shown that no self-expression is art. Such a nonrelative approach renders sensible discussion extinct. The second delusion forgets Barnum & Bailey, Dada, Scriabin, soundtracks (to keep merely within the last four score years). The third delusion ignores the diversity of human nature; some people still thrive on Vivaldi. Mixed media has merely acquired status.

*

Anxiety-stricken concert managers quickly point out that mixed-media groups sell and song recitals don't; they feel that the reason the public buys one is because it doesn't buy the other (a holdover from the one-car-family days when you bought one or the other, never both). The fact is, both managers and recording executives have been coasting on the tried and true for decades and have now reached the bottom of the hill. Who blames passengers for getting off? Since easy money has neither imagination nor responsibility, sooner or later a dead end is reached. But not before a try at cashing in on the *à la mode*.

Major recording labels, which can afford to take chances but say they can't, now promote contemporary music—though only of the far-out (read In) variety—advertising Boulez with the same crass hard-sell that Braniff Airlines uses for Andy Warhol. Such music is thus stamped with the Establishment seal, so the difficult becomes safe. Small companies like Desto, that cannot afford to take chances but do so anyway, are the only ones to record music of the so-called conservative (read tuneful) variety. Such music is thus necessarily adventurous, so simplicity becomes dangerous. If simplicity in "serious" music is eschewed by the avant-garde establishment, it is nonetheless the key to the best of our "avant-garde" rock, which is all that seems to matter anymore. But the best is ever rarer.

*

Like the jaded lover, the jaded music-fancier is one who too often has been forced to react in mediocre situations. At least once a day some friend exclaims, "Now hear *this*," as he puts on the first (and often last) platter by the "Swinging Doors" or the "Conniption Fit." Memory is a curse when revealing this week's totally different beat, sound, or volume distortion as merely the same old beat, sound, or volume distortion we begged the cab driver to turn off last week. The listener is jaded because his ears are literally, *medically*, in trouble.

My first article on the Beatles resulted from an appreciation for their quality. Quality was their originality, and as always quality transcended genre. Since the appearance of that article certain editors imagine me a Pop authority. But that scene only interested me during the brief moment when it contained *the pleasure of quality*. Until such a moment comes again I'll bide my time, as during the arid era between Billie Holiday and the Beatles.

*

It is no accident that the emergence of professional criticism as the preeminent literary form coincided with the rise of amateurism in the other arts. As current criticism feeds on the work of others even by denying that work, so current amateurism feeds off the past even by denying the past—a denial which becomes an end in itself. The cause of this dual rise (descent, really) is, of course, the worsening world situation. This situation has advanced scientific investigation, for better or worse, and the concomitant displacement of artists by scientists who are now possibly our best "creative" minds. Art is both mirror and antidote: it reflects the surroundings, then renders them bearable. A resolution to the sad Vietnam adventure may herald a renaissance as fructuous as the one after World War II. But we will no longer be adolescents.

7

The More Things Change

Notes on French Popular Song

August, 1968.

Paralyzing heat wave. It has been a long time since I visited Paris. The intervening years blur with questions. Is that city's present musical art joined to the undifferentiated internationalism? Do we Americans look in that direction anymore? If we don't, is it because (as older generations always hasten to affirm) things over there aren't what they used to be? or contrariwise, because things there are safely unaltered, while we meanwhile have changed?

The twenties, and again the mid-forties, witnessed mass emigrations to France by sensitive moneyless young Americans in quest of what they called their roots. Youths of the sixties, though richer, stay here. They stay because their roots never were abroad, but deep in home soil turned fertile with autonomous culture. Being older, our young no longer need to run away. Nor do they care much anymore about French doings, except politically.

So with sudden poignance comes the realization that

I too am unaware of musical France today. But, although withdrawn, I do still care.

The French are not a musical people. They are more geared to the eye than to the ear. We too, when thinking of France, usually think less of her sound than her look: her painting and elegant clothes, even her grocery displays delight us. And we also think of her conversation—her exquisitely economical literary wit (not to mention her taste and smell, her cuisine and perfume).

Which is not to say France never produced great musicians: from Machaut to Messiaen, from Adam de la Halle to Jacques Brel, her composers equal any our world has known. But France—the France, that is, of post-World War II—possesses no hard-core musical public; her most adventuresome musicians must cross the border to earn their keep, at least those (composer and performer alike) who make so-called serious music. So-called popular musicians, being less adventuresome, seldom stray; they have always been nourished at home by an audience more concerned with the "visual literature" of their lyrics than with the fairly conventional tunes illustrating those lyrics.

Since that audience's concern would appear unchanged in the France of today, it becomes my concern, my subject, a subject necessarily depicted through comparison. Comparisons are odious when proving similarities between the musical aims of one country and another, then demonstrating that one succeeds where the other fails. But comparisons are fragrant when pinpointing native differences. We are not all the same. Indigenously there is no such thing as better, only different. Dissimilarities have always been what appealingly characterize the nations of our planet. If in recent years many such nations seem menaced by an increase in homogeneity, much of it stamped with the new American "fertile autonomous (!) culture" mentioned above, France has pretty much steered clear.

*

Crass generalities! Perhaps I was sun-struck, for the heat continues. More likely it was habit—the usage of generality picked up from the French who use nothing but. But they counterbalance that use by not expecting to be taken literally (just as I do not literally mean this sentence). Habit turns to style, forcing me to continue in a tone of the general French public.

*

If the general French public is not musical especially, specialists within the specialty—doubtless from resultant economic requirements—have always been less specialized, more Renaissancy, than their American counterparts. A very serious composer like Poulenc, or Henri Sauguet, will one day compose a strong Mass for chorus and orchestra, next day a fragile waltz for Yvonne Printemps. He thus follows the practice of Satie before him, of Reynaldo Hahn before Satie, of Messager before Reynaldo Hahn, Chabrier before Messager, and so on back. Or take Georges Auric who, after years of creating obscure ballets for Diagheleff, or of writing sonatas and such along with some thirty film scores nobody ever listened to, finally struck it really rich with the ditty *Moulin Rouge*.

As for executants, consider Jeanne Moreau. She began in the 1940's as a bilingual (her mother was English) vocalist with Ray Ventura's band before going straight as an actress in Vilar's left-wing troupe, from whence she graduated into everyone's favorite neurotic movie star—who still records unneurotic songs, mostly by the innocuous Cyrus Bassiak. Meanwhile casual balladeers like Brel, drunk with success, branch into oratorio (with less success), while *chansonnier* Yves Montand has largely renounced singing to become one of his country's major stage and screen actors. Actor Serge Reggiani reverses Montand's route by now offering pleasant recitals in vaudeville. Jean Marais does that too, and so does Bardot. (The French, by the way, never use "our" word vaudeville—that form of entertainment extinct here but vital in Paris where ironically it's called *le music-hall*.)

Of course many American composers, long-haired and short, have also worked in many mediums, and certainly the performing versatility of a Sinatra or a Doris Day will raise our eyebrows in various directions. But these are exceptions to our rule of specialized rigors.

*

Specialized also, and quite inflexible, have been both form and matter of American popular song from Stephen Foster until just recently. Standard Tin Pan Alley layout was the thirty-two measure A-B-A, inevitably in a 4/4 meter—the dance of innocence—leading us in a circle. The chief tune, A, stated twice in eight-measure bars, led to an unmemorable bridge built on eight new bars, then back again to a third and final and literal emphasis of the tune. The tune, then, thrice reiterated, is what we remembered more than the words which, in evoking those moons of love or Junes of lovelessness, betrayed a static state of body.

Fluid states of mind are what French popular songs portray: they have always told stories that develop in a straight line, A-B-C, toward a delicious or catastrophic resolution. Which is why their words haunt us more than their melodies. French song is thus not bound to set forms: the subject imposes the pattern. Often the meter shifts to (or is entirely within) a regular 3/4 —the dance of experience.

In storytelling lies the key to France's musical variety, from the *trouvères* to the modern minstrels. If, from Ronsard to Eluard, her great bards have not always been composers in their own right, modern composers—classical and popular—have always used their poetry. But they write their own too. That typically gallic phenomenon called *auteur compositeur* is as persuasive today as the new *auteurs cinéastes* who invent films in transit. Like Elizabethan playwrights they sell to every public; not for nothing does the prestigious series, *Poètes d'Aujourd'hui*, publish as pure poetry the lyrics of vulgar songsters like Brassens, Aznavour, or even Charles Trenet, alongside Mallarmé, Pasternak, or Paul Claudel. (Claudel too was a general practitioner, being not only a poet but a leading dramatist and foreign diplomat. Imagine that in America: the collected verse of maybe Bob Dylan coming out in *Modern Library* coincidentally with his nomination as ambassador to Tokyo!)

*

Those pedagogical opinions were determined, rightly or otherwise, during a decade abroad. Opinions shift with the times, harden to conclusions or melt into reflections, then finally change. But change? *Plus ça change plus c'est la même chose*, as the French are the first to observe: the more things change, the more they revolve back to their starting point. Revolution (as opposed to revolt) is everywhere traditional; my musical opinions, after a long flow of learning, now return on the wings of unaltered taste to when I was learning firsthand about Paris.

*

I arrived there nineteen years ago, the day world champion Marcel Cerdan was killed in a plane crash. The same crash claimed violinist Ginette Neveu, and these two idols, different as night from day, were mourned together.

The French love their intellectual and popular heroes, and are loyal to both without distinguishing much between them. The humblest concierge, while he may identify more with the sagas of Fernandel, is proud to cite Debussy or Balzac; he may not know their works but he'll name a street for them. Culture was never a dirty word in Europe; in America the rare genuinely accepted culture heroes, as embodied in a Hemingway or an Orson Welles, were known for their *bon vivantisme* and not for what their art represented. In those good old 1940's, as in the days of Louis Quatorze, all

France was aware of the privacy of her most public citizens. When Americans were not allowed then to consider their statesmen as having mistresses (or worse), the French followed with relish and approbation the anxieties and bedroom triumphs of the great. (Today, with de Gaulle and the Kennedys, the situation is somewhat reversed.)

So two masters, one of the boxing ring, the other of the concert stage, were conjointly lamented, as later Colette and Mistinguett would be, Gide and Louis Jouvet, Poulenc and Gérard Philipe. And on that awful October Friday of 1963 when Jean Cocteau and Edith Piaf fell dead, hand in hand so to speak, the rule was ironically reaffirmed. Cocteau, a jack-of-all-higher-trades, had been the esoteric darling of the elite. Piaf, a specialist of commoner emotions, had been the pathetic oracle of the workingman. Yet Cocteau had composed monologues for Piaf who, in turn, was Cerdan's mistress at the time of the boxer's death. Which brought the unhappy family about full circle.

At the time of my arrival Piaf was becoming her country's official widow. Humor, never her strong point, now utterly quit the repertory as her every private moan swelled into a public dirge, a culminating dirge of such importance that, despite the continuing New York heat of today, I'd like, before discussing other past and present French singers, to set their stage with this particular woman, my first and longest continental infatuation, *la môme*—as her countrymen called her—the little sparrow.

She was the greatest popular singer produced by France in this century. Of the genre she became an apex, and as such proved—while remaining utterly

French—an exception to the French practice of non-specialization.

The genre, of course, was the troubadour epic which ultimately evolved into the naturalistic *fin de siècle* café-concert narrations of Yvette Guilbert, a sort of contralto whose piquant physique was glorified by Lautrec as early as 1890, and whose bizarre vocality she herself engraved on wax as late as the mid-thirties. (But she died in only 1944, seven years after our Bessie Smith. Why, some of us could have known her!)

Piaf became an apex in that she stemmed directly from Guilbert, through Damia, and like those ladies used song successfully—at least for a time—as a weapon against life. Sharpening their best qualities into a perfect arrow, she pierced the hearts of literally all ensuing Parisian stylists, female and male, except maybe the late French rock crop who aren't really very French.

The utter Frenchness of Piaf came, negatively, through avoidance of Americanisms. If her accompaniments sometimes did insist on a Harlemesque "beat" plus an occasional saxophone (though let's not forget: the saxophone was invented in France a century ago), mostly her orchestrations emulated the oh-so-Latin accordions of the neighborhood *bal musette*. (Incidentally, France's "serious" composers, who always deemed Negro jazz the sole American product worth acknowledging, never managed, from Ravel to Milhaud, more than a translation of the outer trappings into their pristine counterfeits. But then in turn, we never found the key to their kitchen. Like cooking, music is not a universal language.) More positively, Edith Piaf's Frenchness came through the kind of tale she told. If Chevalier at eighty is still (understandably) his nation's official optimist, Piaf, during her forty-four brief years of consoling the urban underdog, represented the *grande pathétique*. Her verses spoke of love fermenting into murder, then of redemption and of love's return in heaven. They spoke of Sunday fairs in the squalid Vincennes park as reward for the barmaid's six-day week. They spoke of injustice in Pigalle's underworld—what Parisians call *le milieu*. They told also, like Jerome Kern's song *Bill*, of life sustained through fidelity to the unfaithful, but, unlike *Bill*, that life was prolonged more through words than music. More as *littérateuse* than as *musicienne* is the sparrow recalled today, as she was applauded in her prime.

As for evading the rule of nonspecialist, Piaf was indeed forever one-track-minded. The concentration made her unique. No *auteur compositeur*, she executed what others (mainly her friend Marguerite Monnot) created so accurately around her private experience of resigned—and not so resigned—distress. This she reexperienced publicly through the *chanson*, an art traditionally depicting city rather than rural problems through a form as valid as (and older than) the recital song as realized by Duparc, say, or Hugo Wolf. Of course, being famous, she was frequently called upon to reenact her number within trumped-up tales for theatre and screen, though she never brought it off. Whatever her number, it was not versatility.

*

This morning I played some early Ethel Merman records, alternating them with Piaf, and with another old and faithful love, Billie Holiday.

Merman belted solely as a technique: she was objective where Piaf was personal. Piaf could belt like Merman, but she melted Merman's brass into the pathos of Holiday.

In more ways than one Edith paralleled Billie. Professionally, though highly mannered vocally (manners, after all, are what make the great great, great being the quality of the inimitably imitable), neither had the least *mannerism* in stage comportment. They just stood there and sang, each in her invariable costume: for Billie the coiffed gardenia, for Edith the simple black dress. Oh, in moments of high emphasis Holiday might close her eyes, while Piaf would slightly raise an arm, as Lenya does, with the tragic simplicity that crumbles mountains; beyond that, nothing—nothing but the immutability of projection. They never "put over" a song other than through the song itself, a lesson our Tony Bennett or Johnny Mathis—to name but two—could nicely heed, inasmuch as they've learned more from women vocalists than from men.

Their personal lives intertwined as well, like Baudelaire's with Poe's, though they may never have heard of each other. Both emerged from the *bas fonds*, Piaf as blind adolescent crooning for pennies in suburban alleys, Holiday as pubescent Baltimore Oriole working the bars of Lenox Avenue. Both their repertories forever featured those youthful and apparently continuing hardships, though Billie became a millionaire and Edith's eventual bridesmaid was Marlene Dietrich. From first to last, though sometimes wealthy and all times beloved, both were victimized and exploited, as is ever the case with simple addicted geniuses whose hearts rule their heads. Both sank back into publicized poverty. Then both perished, early and accidentally, in the icy light of abject stardom.

*

Returning to the Paris of '49 where Piaf reigned supreme, we find certain gentlemen and ladies-in-waiting, no longer waiting.

I asked about suave Jean Sablon, and was told he was passé. (Though just now, in 1968, he's made another record: the French *are* faithful to their heroes!) But the very young and strangely gorgeous Juliette Gréco, yard-long tresses trailing over her slacks, was philosophizing in a Dietrich-like baritone about growing old, on words of Queneau and music of Kosma. Gréco's obsession echoed through the *boîtes* of Saint-Germain where she was crowned high priestess of a superficial Existentialism—to Sartre's dismay. Not to be outdone, Cocteau took her up as he had Piaf, and cast her as a fury in his movie *Orphée*. Then, publicizing the alteration of her handsome nose by stylish Docteur Claoué, she proceeded (still gorgeous though less strange) toward a more standard film career, toward two or three marriages, an affair with Darryl Zanuck whose promotion of her never caught on internationally, a waning of acting demands, and a return to the clubs—this time interpreting material written for her by the rising Françoise Sagan.

I also asked about famous-legged Mistinguett, first mentor and mistress of Maurice Chevalier, and learned she was running a zoo—a *zoo!*—on the route to Saint Tropez. (Though a few years later, well into her seven-

ties, she made a gala comeback: "Her voice still tintin-
nabulates on pitch like a nice weathered sheep bell,"
wrote Janet Flanner.) But the very robust and juvenile
Yves Montand, a protégé of Madame Piaf, was packing
them in at the Théâtre Wagram (since torn down)
with lyrical recitations debonair and earthy on words
by all from Rimbaud to Trenet—and naturally himself.
He grew more somber, more political (left), on wedding Simone Signoret with whom he starred in Sartre's
adaptation of *The Crucible* after triumphing in his first
nonsinging screen role, *The Wages of Fear*.

Around Montparnasse the legendary *diseuse*, Mari-
anne Oswald, still gave lectures on surrealism, acted
in art movies like Kenneth Anger's never-finished *Mal-
doror*, and sang in a voice that made Marlene's sound
like Tebaldi.

Up in Montmartre, Patachou, another old girl friend
of Chevalier, held forth at a special club. In a gentle
voice she interpreted poetry of a compassionate nature,
while wielding a pair of scissors that snipped off the
ties of all male guests (and we know what *that* means).
Next door in her own shop, Geneviève, with an impact
at once tough and tender, declaimed poems anti-war
and pro-love, healthier by bourgeois standards than the
pro-death eulogies heard in left-bank lesbian *boîtes*.

In the mid-1950's younger women such as Mike
Michelle sailed briefly into sight on the reputation of a
single song (like our Bobbie Gentry), then faded out
again.

Younger men lasted longer. And they were blooming
all over, fresh and inventive, composing songs for
themselves and for each other, on words by the classic

French poets or by themselves or by each other. (Stung by the bug, I even wrote a few myself, on the Prévert-oriented poetry of actor Daniel Gélin for Algerian *chanteur* Mouloudji—who never sang them.)

Their tunes mostly leaned toward folk song as synthesized by hotel bands of the 1930's. In beauty of curve few could compare to Richard Rodgers or to the best of the Beatles today. But their words were exhilarating, timely, personal. They sang of their first communion; of sensual discovery during military service in Indo-China; of fantasies—like those of Kafka, Buzzati, Cavafy—about barbarian invasions of Paris streets. Paris streets, down to the last cranny, have always been extolled by their inhabitants with affection or loathing, something seldom done musically for the byways of New York.

In vocal delivery they tended to imitate each other (as Dean Martin and Sammy Davis logically do), or their immediate forerunners like Georges Brassens and Leo Ferré on one hand, Sablon and Trenet on the other. These men were no chickens (neither are Martin and Davis today), though they remained fairly active and very influential. Trenet and Sablon were Crosby-type crooners, while Ferré and Brassens, though doubtless self-styled as "naturalists," had both inherited by osmosis the excruciating nasal vibrato considered elegant by French opera stars. All were troubadours, terribly subjective and quite healthily masculine, endowed with aggressivity and wit, though necessarily short on morbidity and camp.

Who were they? Charles Aznavour, Jacques Brel of course, and the young Gilbert Bécaud. Also youths like

Sammy Frey, Sascha Distel, and a whimsical quartet called the Frères Jacques.

The late fifties saw the distaff side regaining hold with Jacquéline François, Barbara, and the dynamic Germaine Montéro who imposed the raw tint of her native Spain onto the blasé molds of café song.

By 1960 Elvis Presley had so disarmed the rest of the world that France, seldom acquiescent in matters experimental, did open her gates to *le rock-n-roll*, albeit an ersatz version later called Yé Yé. As exemplified in Johnny Halliday this version momentarily immunized Paris against all other music.

In November, 1961, the evening before I left France, Nora Auric (Georges' bright wife) took me to hear Johnny at the Olympia. Still ignorant of Presley—of Presley's *art*, if you will—I was skeptical about meeting it second hand. Yet from the moment that handsome kid appeared, and for the solid hour of his gyrations, Nora and I were as drugged by the mass hysteria loosened by his superbly whorish musicality as were the five thousand adolescents that jammed the hall.

Since then, at least one serious novel has been devoted to Halliday, and a good deal of intellectual criticism. I believe he married his vapid colleague, Sylvie Vartan, then took up with Brigitte Bardot—old enough to be at least his sister. But of these and other things Parisian, most of what I now know I read in women's magazines.

*

This afternoon a responsibility for being *au courant* dragged me through the furnace of Manhattan to the

Discophile where I purchased no less than seventeen newish French records. In a single sweaty séance I listened carefully, and with very mixed reactions, to each and every one. Judging from just these discs, my premise is reconfirmed: the tone of France's forties remains inviolable.

It's sort of comfortable—the realization that in our animated epoch France preserves a snug, almost smug, status quo. She never really did export her art; what we liked of it we robbed, kept provisionally, and gave back. If sometimes the Waldorf or Plaza did extend formal invitations to Gréco or Geneviève, their special impact never "took"; their language lacked that Esperanto appeal of our Westerns ever popular at Champs-Elysées cinemas. Conversely, expatriate Negroes of the 1950's never took, as Josephine Baker had in the 1920's, because they were doing an American thing, while Baker had literally translated her whole being into French. The French did love Negroes as novelty—not as USA exports like Billie Holiday, but as African stylists like Katherine Dunham.

In her isolation France has kept pure. Or almost. She may be different from the USA, but over the years she doesn't grow too different from herself: the fatigue of homogeneity vaguely contaminates her popular music now. Half of it is recorded live in music halls complete with the detestable practice of incorporating the applause. All of it of course is vocal, expressing the good old Gallic themes of putting down the church (yet concerned that if Christ were recrucified today he would pass unnoticed), of putting down the upper classes (to the delight of the chief public, a solvent bourgeoisie), and of putting down old age (though isn't it we Americans who are supposed to be notorious youth-worshipers?). They do still hold love high, and that is a blessing, a blessing of the strictly one-to-one male-female ratio, sometimes garnished with the complacence of longevity, more often with the anxiety of impermanence. Not for Frenchmen the checkerboard possibilities of a tribal Love-in! They reiterate comparatively simplistic problems, old-fashioned I suppose, next to which Anglo-Saxon rock comes off as actually sophisticated. (How long rock will remain sophisticated before sounding old-fashioned is an open question.)

Meanwhile the themes, as uttered on these records, do not activate the present—at least not for me. They reactivate the past.

*

I used never to weep at "great" art, at Couperin or Kierkegaard, maintaining it was too multidimensional for the specific of tears. I wept at the rapid associative revelations of a Piaf, or at Lana Turner's soapy dilemmas. Crying was caused hence by entertainment, not masterworks.

Today tears dictate my first judgment of any works, their levels be damned. What counts is to be kinetically moved. And who says Edith and Lana aren't art—or, if they are, that Kierkegaard is more so? My criterion is no longer analytical.

None of these records makes me weep. They all project a certain hardness, even in heartbreak, which I never used to notice. Maybe their strong level-headedness, compared to our distracted neuroses, goes against the American grain. More likely it's their persistent cliché.

Not one French popular singer of either sex has a real voice, in the sense that our Sinatras or Streisands are real baritones or sopranos. They still "talk" their tunes, beguiling through anecdote rather than through a formal development of sound. Thus their orchestral arrangements strike us as outmoded, naïve. For example, when working toward a climax (and most French songs, being stories, have marked climaxes), they all employ one and only one device: the obvious modulation upward by half-step with each stanza, gaining momentum not through musical invention but by yelling louder. This is as true of the artists of 1968 as of those from 1949, the majority of whom are the same.

*

Juliette Gréco is still very much about, still admired for her philosophic laments, still handsome in her forties while intoning the hit that launched her two decades ago, *Si tu t'imagines*, about youth that can't last. Meanwhile Barbara recounts an older woman's anguish in falling for an adolescent boy. That boy may be Reggiani (now forty-fivish) singing about the "older" woman in his bed, while at other times his frightful touching tenor relates his own problems of aging, put into words by Boris Vian, Apollinaire, and yes, even Baudelaire. Patachou, newly blonde and more than slightly wrinkled, still ingratiates with that calm and not unpleasant hum.

They say Brassens is getting old—a breathing monument—but he still charms dévotés with a vocal monochrome (to me, charmless) whose chief idiosyncrasy remains its lack of idiosyncrasy. And still growing strong in their middle years are Brel and Aznavour; so is Bécaud in his advancing youth.

Of course Aznavour, like Jeanne Moreau, has been internationally immortalized as an actor by new-wave genius François Truffaut. But he sure keeps on singing, or rather, non-singing in his torturous tremolo, forcing the Big Sell as cymbals crash and audience shrieks. Bécaud too continues his non-singing, equally "belovèd" (I cringe when, like Mitch Miller, he invites us fans to join in), and creating grand numbers of which at least one became a hit here last year under the quaintly misconstrued title *It Must Be Him.*

As for Brel, his work too has lately satisfied a certain New York audience, thanks to that curious miscalculation over on Bleecker Street—a disparate black & white version of Brel's own technicolor rendition of his tunes. Those tunes, like virtually all these French ones I've been listening to, are undistinguished, and their instrumental adornments ever more vulgar—meaning literal: they Mickey Mouse the words. The words of Brel I find pretentious because, in deriving from Villon via Kurt Weill and Brecht (in themselves quite noble influences), he takes their sense without their sensitivity, their surface passion without their understatement. Good intentions, honesty, a no-nonsense attitude are not enough for a good song.

The no-nonsense syndrome is all too characteristic of the virile French. They do have guts, if you like guts; but the Brel-Bécaud-Aznavour sound of the confident belligerent male is in complete opposition to the current pop Anglo-American sympathetic adorable sexless cool sound of the Beatles or Tiny Tim. If the French individual extroverts direct their message toward the opposite sex in particular, our collective narcissists direct theirs toward people in general. Americans don't tell stories because gangs don't tell stories, they sing hymns. Stories are what McLuhan would call a hot medium for single singers.

A new record of old Ferré enforces the syndrome. Nonetheless, one of his songs nearly made me cry tonight. *Vingt Ans* examines the same insouciant virtues of youth that Gréco mourns, but where Gréco retains an urbane *sang froid* poor Ferré collapses with a contagious spasm. In another, *Y'en a marre*, the verses hysterically lacerate that same Tax Man the Beatles disdain with a dead pan. Its harmonies, by the way, are right out of Golaud's lament in the last act of *Pélléas* (or Rodolfo's in act three of *Bohème*, which is the same thing), thereby emphasizing a predictable allegiance to an Opéra Comique past rather than to an off-Broadway future. And why not?

Elbowing their way beyond these established rocks into the ebbing starlight of Johnny Halliday's pseudorock are younger boys like Adamo, Antoine, Guy Béart. Cute Sylvie Vartan may still be around, I wouldn't know, but not in competition with post-Piaf kids like Eva, Gribouille, or Mireille Matthieu, assertive little screamers indistinguishable from their predecessor in all but quality.

From far away my impression is that this youthful

clan is less a pastiche of foreign trends than a parasite of the firmly entrenched middle-aged raconteurs. In itself the clan amounts to little, and is certainly not "new." The new in France lies, as always, in tradition: in a refurbishing of the old.

*

New sounds are not perforce more rewarding than old sounds reissued through new media. Not for nothing was *The Umbrellas of Cherbourg*, in all its corny glory, the most satisfying opera produced by any country in a decade. The breakthrough (as they say in advanced circles) lay not in the luscious melodies of Michel Legrand nor in Jacques Demy's tear-jerking libretto, but in the function of these nineteenth-century concepts within a twentieth-century medium. To my knowledge these artists are the first to compose opera directly for film.

If, as suggested earlier, an abstract *enfant terrible* like Pierre Boulez was forced to preach his original gospel beyond homeland borders, the conservative tune-smith Legrand, with his brand new mixture of very conventional materials, has cooked up a serious opera appetizing not only to the common Frenchman, but internationally. And that, once more, by telling a story through song!

Reactionary though the conclusion appears, it would be amusing if France were to become reestablished in her traditional role of avant-garde, not through persistence in the "new" sounds so many of us have wearied of, but through invention of new uses for the tried and true. In finding a modern musical outlet for the old storyteller, the unlimited potential of opera-as-movie has finally been tapped by the French.

*

Have these pages been a bit short on verifiable information? Still, information—or at least instruction—does not come through facts, but through attitude toward facts, and God knows I've attitudinized. Notes like these, if formulated about America for a Parisian monthly, could, like the present vivid heat wave, be obsolete before publication. But France moves more slowly, her traditions are deeper, her heroes last longer. She does indeed love those heroes, for better or worse —*tant bien que mal*. And so, *tant bien que mal*, do I.

These opinions have not got things off my mind, but got them on, making me miss Paris terribly. Nevertheless I am relieved. And the heat has broken.

8

Sun

WHAT a work of art says, and what its maker says it says, need not jibe. Critics will tack on meanings after the fact, that's their job. An artist who supplies meanings cheats.

To offer a technical analysis of his work is for an artist to repeat himself, but with less eloquence. To dismantle a structure is to divulge uninteresting secrets, secrets which he half forgets once the work is done. Even if he could recall each compositional process, to reveal this would be to kiss and tell, like psychotherapy.

For a composer—at least this composer—just having his piece played in public is an embarrassment (albeit sometimes a rewarding embarrassment). Discussion afterward insults the delicious injury. Although I've a point of view toward music, I've no point of view toward *my* music, since I'm not outside looking in. Nor have I an outlook, since the music is its own outlook. Nor have I a philosophy of song writing: if I had I wouldn't write songs but would write philosophy. Furthermore, no composer can even possibly conjecture what distinguishes his music from that of others, other than (hopefully) its quality. Conscious influences he will not readily admit to. Unconscious ones, by definition invisible to the composer, are apparent only (again hopefully) to critics and presumably musicologists. Thus, only as a musicologist can a composer discuss all music except, for the above reasons, his own.

Which is why my blurbs about my own work, on record jackets or sheet music, do not explain the intent of the piece that's been written, nor even how the piece was written, but only (and I repeat it constantly) how it came to be written.

*

What can be told about music that the music itself can't tell? An artist's state of mind and body during his preoccupation with a given composition is ultimately more interesting (not to say valuable) than his solution to those formal problems he sets up for himself.

Sun is my third work for solo voice and orchestra. In 1950 I composed the suite *Six Irish Poems*, for contralto Nell Tangeman. A few years later *Six Dryden Poems* were composed for coloratura Virginia Fleming. Something for "normal" voice with orchestra therefore seemed tempting, but (since the preceding pieces were seldom performed) I doubt it would have gotten written without a commission from Lincoln Center. The commission came in the form of a phone call from William Schuman two summers ago, and offered the perfect excuse. So, after twelve years' absence from the

genre (though not from the human voice: I'd meanwhile produced four operas and perhaps fifty songs), I
began the present work.

Having just completed a long affair for voice and
piano, *Poems of Love and the Rain*, the indicated need
now seemed for *Songs of Hate and the Sun*. A worship-
ful obsession with our planet's star was evident since
childhood, but had only once been phrased in my music:
Lions, A Dream for Orchestra is a nonverbal illustra-
tion of capture and joyful immolation within a burning
mane, which I likened to an astral force. Of course, no
one would know that if I'd not written program notes.
Now, with *Sun*, came the opportunity for an unequivo-
cal statement through words of my friends, the poets.

Like the other vocal-orchestral works, this one is
cyclic, though not a suite of set numbers; eight poems
are instrumentally blended into a continual movement
of some twenty-five minutes. Supposedly the whole
makes a vague narrative (dawn to dark, then day
again); but mostly I chose words, not as I understood,
but as I felt them. They range from those of an
Egyptian king, through Shakespeare and Blake, the
nineteenth century of Byron and Whitman, to our own
America of the late Roethke, my old friend Paul Goodman (the sociological novelist) and my new friend
Robin Morgan (wife of poet Kenneth Pitchford).

Most of the music was finished before we decided
to engage the engaging Jane Marsh as soloist. Miss
Marsh came to visit Saratoga where, during the summer months of 1966, I had been composing. We went
carefully through the pencil score, and I agreed on
tailoring various passages to her special qualities. This

was not a concession but a professional gesture: music, after all, is composed for performers, and one could wish that they (and their public) would remember that more often.

The composition was completed shortly thereafter, and its orchestration accomplished during a similar period of time, i.e., two months in the winter of that year. If one includes the weeks passed in poetry selection, then the whole procedure was realized over a five-month period, spaced in turn over a year and a half. In those same eighteen months—and sometimes simultaneously with *Sun*—I composed a Concerto Grosso titled *Water Music*, an extended cycle for voice and piano called *Hearing*, a chorus and orchestra suite (commissioned by the Koussevitzky Foundation) named *Letters From Paris*, two dance works (one for Martha Graham, the other for Utah University), and several fair-sized pieces for chorus and organ based on religious texts. I also published two books, wrote a third, and spent a year as guest professor in Salt Lake City. My state of mind was, on the whole, more optimistic than usual (despite the rise and fall of a personal relation); my state of body rather more fluctuating.

This is how *Sun* came to be made. As to how it *was* made, any intelligent critic could examine it with hindsight and provide a clearer technical case for it than the composer now cares about doing.

9

Ladies' Music

THE male of nearly all species is bigger, brighter, more eloquent than the female. Consider the peacock or nightingale, the whale or minnow, the tiger or grizzly bear. There are exceptions: one breed of parrot produces a ruby-hued female, while the male is merely emerald. And in various strains of arachnid, males are not only tinier than their mates: after mating they are devoured and become quite invisible.

But with virtually all mammals, the male is physically more conspicuous than the female. All mammals, that is, except humans.

This is fact. Interpretations vary. That the male is gaudier in appearance does not mean he is quicker in mind; it defines his role as protector who diverts enemies away from the inconspicuous egg-sitter. Yet with certain groups—lions, for instance—the female is the provider. As to whether the lioness is less lovely than her shimmering husband is a question of taste, and a human taste at that. In mankind's high periods of art, simplicity takes precedence over the ornate.

Yet even in the highest periods the human female, through her accouterment, has made herself more visible than the male. Is this her assertion—or is it man's permission—that she is not an animal? Very early woman became, superficially, more brilliant than her masculine counterpart, adopting a wardrobe in simulation (or from the actual skins) of the male animal. If at Louis XIV's court men sported spike heels and twelve-inch perruques, their women bettered them with fifty-foot trains and cages containing live birds woven into their spiraling headdresses. (The stately saraband evolved to accommodate these clothes.) And if in our 1930's female impersonators outdid each other in extravagant drag, again they were one-upped, as Parker Tyler elucidates, by somnambulist marvels like Mae West or Marlene Dietrich who, with their feathers and scarlet fingernails, became impersonators of female impersonators.

Only today, with her ardent emancipation program, does woman revert to what opponents name her natural dowdiness. Men meanwhile, casting off gray flannels for gorgeous robes, inasmuch as they still differ from the other sex, differ from it as flowers differ.

*

Despite what current suffragists contend, women from many points in time and space have been strong in politics: think of Cleopatra of Egypt or Queen Balkis of Sheba, Elizabeth Tudor of England or Catherine II of Russia, Golda Meir of Israel, or Indira Gandhi of India.

Women have been strong in poetry and letters, from

Sappho to Sévigné, from Sand to Stein. Admittedly there's a vast lacuna between 200 B.C. and 1600 A.D.: I can think of only two women writers—both vigorously Christian—during that span: the tenth-century German playwright, Hroswitha, who wrote in Latin, and the sixteenth-century Spanish mystic, Teresa, who wrote in Castilian. But today, at least in the English-speaking world, there are as many top-notch female fictionists—not to mention critics—as male.

Strong, too, have they been in visual art, though for a shorter time. France seems first to have spawned them in the 1800's. Rosa Bonheur immediately comes to mind, then Mary Cassatt and Marie Laurencin in the early twentieth century. At present in America there may be more good women painters than men, and treated just as seriously, that is, getting the same fees.

Our century has also produced scientists, anthropologists, historians, reporters, and precedent-shattering choreographers, impresarios, and theatre specialists as dissimilar as Madame Curie, Margaret Mead, Edith Hamilton, Janet Flanner, Dorothy Day and Dorothy Thompson, Mary Wigman, Jean Rosenthal, and Jean Dalrymple. And our century gave us the philosopher Susanne Langer who has written as knowledgeably *about* music as anyone ever.

Yet she has not written music.

*

Why, when we have seen so many women long excelling in what are commonly thought to be masculine categories, have the few women composers been of such recent vintage?

97

Is it because music, although probably the oldest art, is nevertheless the youngest in that it is the last to have gained individuality (the composer as individual is hardly three centuries old) and thus corresponds to the distaff's tardy emancipation?

Is it then because until modern times music everywhere was predominantly a religious expression, and in the west predominantly Christian, and among Christians predominantly male? If indeed the church is a man's world, before the Renaissance it was musically not even that, but a domain of asexual anonymous contributors.

Is it because, like the theatre (though unlike poetry or sculpture), music is an *interpretive* craft? and women make better interpreters than they do creators, interpretation being artificial, and artifice—use of make-up, of costume, of song—being more socially fitting to girls than boys? Then what of play-acting, that great artifice whose golden peaks in Greece and England eschewed women completely?

Is it because, again like the theatre, there are problems of execution which need never be faced by poets and painters? Music, before it can exist in the ear of an audience, needs a middleman. And any composer, unless he spends his career writing solely for friends who "play piano," will logically be drawn to the orchestra. Now the orchestra is a man's world, autocratic and closed, ruled by an absolute despot. The orchestral players' reaction to all comers, soloist and conductor alike, is one of "you gotta show me." If to them the living composer in general is an object of contempt, the female composer is an object of derision.

On this last point, an esthetic consideration: music, which is sounded and which exists only in performance, is more assertive than pictures which are mute and which exist in themselves, or than poems which are half mute and half sound. Still, the patron saint of music was a woman, the virgin Cecilia who died a Roman martyr eighteen hundred years ago. From that time until the Freudian revolution, music was often termed a feminine art, and thus an art fit only for men to tamper with. If, even today, your typical male composer (and there *is* a type) is less extrovert, less aggressive, than your average male painter, the reason lies elsewhere than in the giddy assumption that the arts they practice embody sexual identity.

*

A rule is not conscious of itself. The white man in a white land seldom thinks of his color, while the Negro in a white land seldom thinks of anything else. By the same token there is no white music when all music is white. Most of what most of us have heard in the western world has been white for three milleniums. For three centuries, however, there has been black music (black, when heard against a white background: the black music of Africa is not black to black Africans). We have absorbed this as slave songs, as spirituals, as jazz, and more recently as an art form by specific conservatory-trained individuals aiming for the concert hall while still (like the best Negro prose, for the moment) using race as subject matter.

Similarly, there is no male music because it is all

male. So unquestioned is the premise that we can afford to patronize rather than resent those females who do enter the arena.

I don't mean the glittering plethora of performing ladies, 90 percent of whom are singers, from Handel's day through Jenny Lind to Bethany Beardslee, with Marguerite Long and Myra Hess at the ivories. Nor do I mean those black women, Ma Rainey, Josephine Baker, Mary Lou Williams, Marian Anderson, Hazel Scott, Mattiwilda Dobbs, who have instituted new traditions with grace and force. Significantly, we don't yet find major black women soloists in the nonvocal "serious" domain—no concert violinists, for example, or pianists—although in orchestras there are some, notably the percussionist Elayne Jones who, ever since I can remember, has been featured in the special recitals of ultramodern music in the New York vicinity.

I mean composers. There are a handful—and none before 1900. (Oh yes, there *are* earlier examples. Pauline Viardot-Garcia, Rossini's soprano virtuoso, did write at least one apparently delightful opera for performance by herself in the 1830's. And a hundred years earlier Bach's second wife, Anna Magdalena, composed a bit, mostly transcriptions. But these, both in intent and effect, are really exercises, albeit distinguished ones.) The early decades showed us Dame Ethel Smyth in Britain, and the Boulanger sisters, Nadia and Lili, in France. France in the twenties brought renown to Germaine Tailleferre, in the thirties to Marcelle de Manziarley, in the forties to Betsy Jolas. America in the forties weaned Miriam Gideon, Louise Talma, Vivian Fine, the black Julia Perry, the Australian-born Peggy Glanville-Hicks, the South African born Elisabeth Lutyens, and the German-born Ursula Mamlok. Today there is an International Society of Women Composers headed by Poland's Grazyna Bace-wicz. All are well-schooled first-rate musicians. Mostly they do not use womanhood as subject matter, and they shudder at the phrase Ladies' Music, a sarcastic classi-fication defensively coined by men during the world-famous popularity of Cécile Chaminade's *Scarf Dance*.

And yet, until around 1950 when the civil rights pot began to boil, we applauded the subtlest gesture of the creative female as we applauded the black—with the condescension accorded to talking dogs.

(When Mormons are challenged about refusing the heavenly priesthood to Negroes, their whimsical ration-ale is: we refuse it also to women.)

*

What happened in 1950? The time-worn ecological scale balancing church and state began toppling, and ten years later splintered irreparably. By church, of course, I mean concert hall, and by state, the clubs and streets and coffee houses. All merged and blurred. Ladies were no longer treated as talking dogs, since all music, including ladies', went to the dogs. Each art, in lowering standards toward mass orientation, coinci-dentally became interchangeable with each other art. Ironically, the older Ladies' Music, high on the crest of a liberation gap, fell into the pollution and drowned, while younger talents of all sexes headed away from art.

*

What is Ladies' Music? It is easier to define this by first defining the more tangible Ladies' Literature:

On the one hand it pretends to be nothing more than what is generally considered feminine (instinctive, fluffy), deals with the so-called female psychology from the inside out, and addresses itself to women readers. At worst it is overdressed, rambling, sensational, and lax, like the prose of Hollywood columnists, *Cosmopolitan*, or Margaret Mitchell. At best it bursts from an enviably tight and tailored yet excruciatingly sensitive cocoon, and soars beyond category, like Virginia Woolf, Willa Cather, or the wonderful women of France from Madame de Lafayette to the all-knowing Colette. Some men write high-quality Ladies' Literature, "poetic" prose, elaborately plotted, dealing nonintellectually with "feminine psychology": Pierre Louÿs, Oscar Wilde, Tennessee Williams. Interestingly, an author like Mary Renault, while involved exclusively with male—especially "inverted" male—sensibility more tellingly than any man, elusively retains her female identity (possibly because she treats inverted love as simply love) through the sixth sense compassionately implied in Jean Paulhan's letter to the pseudonymous and supposedly unknown perpetrator of *Story of O:*

> That you are a woman I have little doubt. Not so much because of the kind of detail you delight in describing—the green satin dresses, wasp-waist corsets, and skirts rolled up a number of turns (like hair rolled up in a curler)—but rather because of something like this: the day when René abandons O to still further torments, she still manages to have

enough presence of mind to notice that her lover's slippers are frayed, and notes that she will have to buy him another pair. To me, such a thought seems unimaginable. It is something a man would never have thought of, or at least would never have dared express.

That paragraph might be a red herring. Responsible rumor maintains Paulhan himself authored the story.

On the other hand, Ladies' Literature may appear so lean of style, so businesslike of content, so precise and yet so deep of insight, so political, in short so masculine, that only a woman could be the originator, no man—not even Hemingway, nor surely Kenneth Burke —feeling *that* impelled to assert his maleness. (It used to be popular to say that Norman Mailer's writing suggested that of a repressed homosexual. Trends change quickly. A cursory reading now of, say, *An American Dream*, shows the narrator to be a reasonably adjusted heterosexual posing as a repressed homosexual.)

Mary McCarthy has been said to perform in manly style, as have Brigid Brophy, Susan Sontag, Hannah Arendt (for nuisance value include Diana Trilling, though not Doris Lessing or Simone de Beauvoir who are too baroque, too longwinded) because the filtering of intelligence and originality through an economical sieve has, until recently, been considered a masculine operation. What is thought to betray these persons as female is a certain willful coldness, though that too is hardly an exclusive terrain: how about the cynicism of G.B.S., Alexander Woollcott, John Simon!

Women no longer hide beneath *nom-de-plumes*, like

the Georges Eliot and Sand. Yet editors, voyeuristic and discriminatory, still consider it appropriate to engage them for mutual criticism. Like Amazons in the Roman arena they overcompensate (Jean Garrigue's review of Anaïs Nin's diary), over-resent (Joyce Carol Oates' report on Janet Frame's novel), or take it upon themselves to defend their less fortunate sisters (Mrs. Trilling's Johnny-come-lately epitaph for Marilyn Monroe). Somehow this all seems unfair, unfair to themselves, since it calls forth their worst writing. They cancel each other out, like poets reviewing each other poetically. They aren't reviewing other people, but other female people. Any meanness involved is interpreted as prejudicial, as though they are *men* writing about women, or whites who aren't yet permitted to dislike certain blacks on purely human terms.

When Virginia Woolf turns her cutting pity on Katherine Mansfield, or Miss McCarthy clarifies, with an understanding surpassing Nathalie Sarraute's, Nathalie Sarraute, they present exceptions proving the rule.

*

Then what is Ladies' Music?

The "meaning" of musical art is more mercurial than the meaning of any other art, so Ladies' Music is harder to define than Ladies' anything else. Substitute Music for Literature in the preceding paragraphs and you will have at least one definition.

Ladies' Music isn't what girls used to enjoy playing, *Rustle of Spring*, Chopin *Nocturnes*, anything Romantic with hands crossed. It is music composed by women who lack not talent but discipline, who aim at a low target like wisteria or a robin's egg and *miss the mark.* As for compensatory male music by women (tough ideas that aim high, like an Iris Murdoch—not a Jane Austen—novel), even if it once could have been identified, it is now, as I've explained, lost in the international monochrome mire.

There are no musical equivalents of fiction and nonfiction, so one cannot claim that women composers, as opposed to any composers, excel in certain genres of music.

*

What is black subject matter? In fiction and essays it is the black life viewed, at present, strictly problematically. In contemporary music it is black folk material (African and American) recast into more complex molds.

What is womanhood as subject matter? In sound it must be the same as in letters, and has sense only in the programmatic or operatic: music depicting a story about a woman. Now, the fact that Louise Talma chose to compose a tragedy about Alcestis, as did Martha Graham (who has also choreographed climaxes in the lives of virtually every female monster from Medea to Emily Dickinson), need not imply that these creators are involved in *women*'s creation any more than Euripides or Racine were so involved. Nor is Miriam Gideon, when setting to music the verses of (Mr.) Francis Thompson, invading a man's territory.

Music is the most sexless of the arts. The meaning of that sentence lies in its meaninglessness. It would be meaningless to contend the same of any "representational" art.

*

Martha Graham, as you gauge such things, is one of the seven geniuses of any sex in any field today. Although genius and innovation do not inevitably go hand in hand, she has influenced change in dance more than any person or group (certainly more than Balanchine) during the past hundred years. Yet her very preoccupation with the female as female, particularly the more-than-criminal female as Royal Elect, would disqualify her from membership in Women's Liberation Front.

Susan Sontag provoked a new approach to thinking —and non-thinking—more forcibly than any man (certainly more than Mailer) during the sixties. Her thesis was good: that all art excites; from this she managed extraordinary cases for ordinary books. Yet more and more she becomes a weight—not a dead weight, but a weight all the same. A camp she is not. Camp is passé anyway, for we are fickle.

We quickly throw art into the mire (art which lowers its standards, along with art that does not), and still more quickly we change criteria for judging that art. One can and does, I suppose, listen to, perhaps, Joan Baez, with tears in the eyes, if that means anything (and it does), which is more than can be said of, perhaps, Karlheinz Stockhausen. Yet when Baez is judged, as she is most often, by judges with tears in their eyes, the judgment disqualifies itself. Young musicians in Stockhausen's milieu write easily but do not listen. In Baez' milieu they listen easily but do not write. It comes to the same thing.

*

With certain women in music the ridiculous is serious. Thus pathetic. Has anyone forgotten the coloratura of Florence Foster Jenkins? Or the cornet of Giullietta Masina in *La Strada?*

During the 1940's, one Mabel McAllister, a blue-haired Texas matron, hired the small Carnegie Recital Hall to perform a program of her own piano works. Her brochure announced, almost as an afterthought, this information: "One fascinating aspect of Mrs. Mc-Allister's compositions is that they are all written exclusively for the black keys."

Last year a London woman received wide acclaim for her communion with dead composers. She took dictation directly from Beethoven, Liszt, and others. Who's to say that the dubious quality of the result was caused by the London woman's lack of talent rather than by the composers' senility?

With men the ridiculous is usually conscious satire. Harpo Marx, Victor Borge. And while some women also display method in their madness—Anna Russell, Jo Stafford—it's difficult to find examples of the converse: men, whose tackiness is innocent. Surely Liberace is not fooled by his image.

If Wanda Landowska, like the London woman, was on close terms with the dead, she also delivered the goods—this, despite elaborate theatrics which, for all we know, were standard nineteenth-century fare. I first saw her in 1944. Emerging onto the stage of Town Hall, she spent a full four minutes gliding slow-motion toward her lamp-lit harpsichord (during which she leered like a snake-charmer at her public whose accompanying applause was undiminishing), sat down upon seven gold pillows, stood up again to remove one pillow which she cast on the floor, reseated herself, poised her right hand to play, froze it in mid-air, replaced it in her lap, and turned again toward us. Long pause. "Last night Johann Sebastian Bach came to me. For several hours we compared the fruits of our mutual study. He then bequeathed to me registrations and fingerings which I will perform, and which you will hear, for the first time this evening." From the audience an abject sigh of thanks, from the stage a recital which practiced what it promised. Hers was the grand authenticity which anticipated, and thus automatically disqualified, all sister-colleagues.

*

The unsolicited verse I receive from poetasters, eager for song settings and (by indirection in their fantasy-logic) avid for fortune, is mostly by women over sixty whose subject matter is the American flag.

*

Still another breed of musical woman is The Composer's Widow. She is usually a naturalized German-American who, though often a musician herself, spends her declining years mainly promoting her late husband's pieces: the Mrs. Weigl, Schillinger, Weill, Itor Kahn, de Hartmann, Mahler, Berg.

*

From the Industrial Revolution until 1950 the artist has commonly been accepted (rejected) as an Alienated Decoration. Art accordingly was the sole ground whereon men and women theoretically met with equality. In fact, as I have tried to show, women suffered discrimination in art, as elsewhere. Less perhaps in the silent arts, painting and writing, which can be practiced "in hiding," than in the noisy ones, theatre and musical performance, which require a personal and assertive presence. Such a presence will be, almost automatically, eccentric, bigger than life, a Streisand, a Leontyne Price, or, against three odds, a black woman playwright like Lorraine Hansberry whose untimely end followed a certain logic.

Why then, finally, so few women in the *creative* musical field? The answer is clear. Whereas poems, even great poems, can be completed in haste at a supermarket or in the maternity ward, and whereas pictures, especially terrible ones, can be drawn by literally anyone from age one to a hundred, because writing and drawing are languages integral to everyone's everyday life, musical composition (great or terrible) is not a language for dabblers. A minimum of professionality and a maximum of time are required to produce a communicable score. If, as is generally conceded, the bringing into existence of a two-hour opera, from conception to production, is a matter of around three years comprised of ten-hour days, days absorbed in the highly technical questions of not only composition but of instrumentation, piano-vocal reduction, supervision of orchestral extraction and copy, interminable conferences and sectional rehearsals, it is hard to picture a woman achieving this proficiency in her art while raising a family with the comparatively unneurotic ease of her sisters "in poetry."

If gift knows no gender, neither does lack of gift. When music reaches, as it threatens, the point of gratuitous simplisticism now reached by other arts, then talent will be more indistinguishable than the sexes have become, and nobody will know, or care, who composed what. Still, that may indicate the route toward an ideal society where, according to Freud, art will no longer be necessary.

10

Around Satie's Socrate

> ". . . a freakish French musician, more inventor than creator, Erik Satie . . ."
> —PAUL LANDORMY,
> *A History of Music*

> "God will not be fooled; He hates literature. He loved the blue eyes of Satie."
> —JACQUES MARITAIN

WHAT used to be termed "modern" becomes, as we know, digestible to laymen when superimposed on other mediums. Audiences swallow without flinching music conjoined to film or ballet, music which in concert would send them off screaming. Yet the famous riots all seem to have dealt with visual or vocal music like *Salomé* or *Pierrot Lunaire*. Are there non-programmatic pieces that have impelled real scandals, other than scandals of boredom? Is it mischievous to suggest that the notorious rumpus at the première of *Le Sacre du Printemps* was provoked less by Stravinsky's score than by Nijinsky's terrible choreography?

*

Advocates of rock and of black folk music, both basically kinetic expressions, discuss the presumed complexity of their art as though complexity were a virtue. Not only is complexity not a virtue (nor a vice), it is not an element of rock or of black folk music. Simplicity is the necessary ingredient, thus the true "virtue," of any music that moves us to song and dance. Complexity deactivates the body—make us *débander*, as the French say—because it stimulates the brain. Counterpoint, by nature abstract and by extension "spiritual," is more complex, at its simplest, than the verbally carnal and squarely rhythmic folk-rock. We don't naturally dance to abstraction. Rhythm, by nature less abstract, *can* lean in that direction: we don't dance convincingly, or at least impulsively, to complicated (read irregular) rhythms. No one has successfully choreographed *Le Sacre*.

Le Sacre has not worked as a ballet because hitherto its choreographers have taken it at face value. (My most recent encounter: those Mickey-Mousing bumps-&-grinds of Béjart's Chosen Virgin.) Any choreography which "explains" music on the music's terms is asking for pulverization. Dance must go against. Try this solution: cocktail-party intrigue with *Le Sacre* as background.

Or choreograph three stories—of ritual murder, of the building of Boulder Dam, of life with Hell's Angels —and use Erik Satie's *Sarabandes*.

*

A triumph in style, among other things, Stravinsky's *Sacre* still sounds as fresh as the day it was born.

This is the way with masterpieces. Yet it's unlikely, though unprovable, that anyone including the composer still hears it as it was heard then.

Now, a masterpiece like Satie's *Socrate*, is, in a sense, without style—without immediate location in time. Thus we probably do hear (and misunderstand) it the same way as on its birthday.

The rule, at least in our century, is that most new pieces sound dated sooner or later. Honegger, for example, or much of Copland. The rare ironic twist is in the piece which when first played sounded old-fashioned, but which now seems original. In America, Moore's *Baby Doe*, Barber's *Knoxville*, Bernstein's *Jeremiah*. In France, much of Poulenc. Though while the intent of the Moore-Barber-Bernstein work remains intact, we now read new motivations into Poulenc: as with Satie, we no longer admit his frivolity to be frivolity.

But we must earn the right to denigrate a master. We must earn the right to denigrate Satie who was not, properly speaking, a master. We must earn the right to declare him overrated, in the face of those who declare him underrated in the face of those who never rated him at all.

*

Since childhood I've known him. His *Gnosiennes*, *Nocturnes*, and *Gymnopédies* joyfully saturated my adolescent keyboard practice long before Chopin displaced them. His *Socrate* is the one piece I've played every day for a decade without getting bored, the pleasure of expectation remaining always new. Then am I granted a right to state that, despite the Cage-Thomson-Milhaud sanction and syndrome (the "in" notion that Satie's undervalued), Satie may indeed be overestimated? (History forbids our pronouncing Beethoven a bore, Casals a Maharishi.) When folks easily declare that nine-tenths of the piano pieces or even *Parade* are silly, inept, unsatisfactory to the ear, we ask: Do you know *Socrate?* No, they answer. Now, *Socrate* is one of our century's five masterworks. Knowing, feeling, this, we may agree that *Parade* and nine-tenths of the piano pieces are unsatisfactory to the ear, inept, silly.

*

Satie never scared anybody. But certainly he did attract and influence his more celebrated peers because of his vitriolic anti-Wagner stance. Indeed, one thinks of Satie as older than Debussy, so great was his hold on the latter who first met him when Satie was earning a living as a café pianist. Actually Satie was born in 1866, four years after Debussy, though nine years before Ravel, both of whom had solid conservatory training and ultimately a fame far wider than their friend's. At age forty, when someone told Satie his music lacked form, he did apply for study with d'Indy, after which he composed his famous *Pièces en forme d'une Poire*. There began his series of cute titles, mostly defensive, one must conclude, since the music itself was seldom more cute than the Rosicrucian ritual which had previously influenced it. Knowledge, training, do not of themselves make a better, fuller artist.

The artist always finds before he seeks. Like Schubert, Satie knew as much as he needed to know to extract from himself what there was to extract and then write it down. His go at the Conservatoire in no way advanced him beyond his poignant titles. . . . Like everyone else, he became associated with Diagheleff during the teens of our century, collaborating with Picasso on two ballets, *Mercure* and *Parade,* the latter with a scenario by the young Jean Cocteau. He and Cocteau were eventually to become the father and mother of that twenties group who, for a while, called themselves *Les Six:* Germaine Tailleferre, Louis Durey, Francis Poulenc, Arthur Honegger, Darius Milhaud, Georges Auric. Toward the end of his life, another group of his disciples (including Roger Désormière and Henri Sauguet) became known as the Arceuil School. Socially Satie was a wag, domestically a recluse.

*

A composer's composer. More exactly, a Francophile composer's composer, meaning he never played in those waves of colorful virtuosity which attract even the most sophisticated amateur, not to mention performer. His Frenchness lay in economy and wit, often lightweight though never dull. His music, more like drawing than like painting, gave, said Cocteau, more than it promised. "Satie protected his music like good wine; he never shook the bottle."

His philosophy, in relating the conventionally unrelated (equating wit with sorrow as a qualitative expres-

115

sion, for instance) was not far from today's pop culture which makes the ordinary extraordinary by removing it from context. Elsewhere, conversely, like the surrealists, he treated his eccentric subject-matter straightforwardly. Between the lines and among the notes of his compositions he often inserted little jokes, whimsical advice to the performer, or "impossible" directions not unlike those Charles Ives was employing at the same time in America. No one would think of taking him literally. (When John Cage rented the old Living Theatre for a presentation of Satie's *Vexations* —a short piano work concluding with the words: repeat 472 times—hiring a relay of pianists to play the piece consecutively for sixteen hours, he produced a Cageian, not a Satiesque, experience.)

*

Erik Satie's greatest work by far is *Socrate*, commissioned in 1919 by the Princesse Edmonde de Polignac, and composed originally for small orchestra with several human voices (which, however, never sing in ensemble). An equally, perhaps more, persuasive version is for solo voice and piano.

Socrate takes just over half an hour: fairly long as pieces go; as a program in itself, fairly short. Yet it is a totality, standing best alone. Nothing seems to "go" with it, least of all other works by Satie since, in a way, they are all contained within *Socrate*.

*

The texts chosen by Satie for his music were, of all things, from Plato's *Dialogues*, highly truncated and in French translation by one Victor Cousin of the Sorbonne. These the composer set to music without romantic affectation, even without vocal embellishment, but almost as they would be spoken. He set them, literally so to speak, with respect. Respect—that is, humility—is not a quality one especially associates with genius. Yet humility is precisely the genius of *Socrate:* the words of Plato are not illustrated, not interpreted, by the music: they are framed by the music, and the frame is not a period piece; rather, it is from all periods. Which is what makes the music so difficult to identify. Is it from modern France? ancient Greece? or from the time of Pope Gregory?

I've said *Socrate* is one of the few pieces to which for two decades I've repeatedly returned without disappointment, the pleasures of anticipation remaining always fresh. But as this anticipation is not contained in highs and lows, for newcomers the music can feel static. In the academic sense *Socrate* has no development beyond the normal evolution imposed by the text. Hence the music moving forward seldom relates to itself thematically, though its texture remains almost constantly undifferentiated. The dynamic level never rises above mezzo-forte, with little contrast and virtually no climax until the final page when we hear forty-four inexorable knellings of an open fifth which denote the agony of Socrates who, in the last two bars, expires with a sigh. The harmony, mostly triadic, is rarely dissonant, and never dissonant in an out-of-key sense except in a single "pictorial" section, again from the end movement, when the jailer presses Socrates' legs which have grown heavy and cold from the hemlock: here the words are colored with repetitions of a numbingly foreign C-sharp.

Wherein lies the genius, the ever-renewed thrill of expectation? It lies in the composer's absolutely original way with the tried and true. The music is not "ahead" of its time, but rather (and of what other work can this be said?) outside of time, allowing the old, old dialogues of Plato to sound so always new.

11

Bill Flanagan

1923-1969

Nagged by that awful question: do you consider yourself foremost a writer or a musician?, he of course answered: a musician. For, like myself, Bill Flanagan became an author by virtue of whatever reputation he had earned as a composer, not the other way around.

We were the same age, and of similar convictions, namely that there was still blood in tonality, breath in the simple line, and that the flesh of music could be grafted onto the skeleton of poetry and given life by the singing voice, with a feeling of heightened naturalness for the listener. We remained close, if competitive, allies for twenty-three years. During some of those years we presented a very popular series, the Rorem-Flanagan concerts, of vocal music by Americans.

A decade ago, for the bulletin of the American Composers Alliance, at Flanagan's invitation and with his blessing, I wrote a survey examining virtually all of his compositions, relating them to his working habits, and those habits to his life pattern. His output up to then had been small by any standard: less than three hours of music produced over fourteen fairly active years. During the nine years that remained of his life, Bill composed proportionately even less: about a half-hour's worth of completed score. Since this remainder does little to alter the survey, I have no more to add by way of analysis about Flanagan the creator. His catalogue, for better or worse, is closed.

About Flanagan the man we all will speculate indefinitely. He was much more complicated than his music. Like his songs he was sad, but he was more intelligent than they—if one can speak of songs as, in themselves, containing intelligence. His perceptions were diamond hard; his logical, original, Jesuit-trained mind was such that very little escaped it. Very little except, of course, himself. His real body, which drank at West Village bars, could not keep pace with his fantasy of that body, which drank at the fountain of youth. He literally danced himself to death. As the action, or rather non-action, of the hero in his opera *Bartleby* set the tone for much of Flanagan's own life style, so the contagious tune in his *Illic Jacet* foresang his death: ". . . in love with the grave./And far from his friends and his lovers/He lies with the sweetheart he chose."

I used to be embarrassed by discussions about the waste of an artist's life cut short. (Remarks like "If only Schubert had lived, think of the beauty he would have bequeathed!" sound presumptuous.) I used to think artists died when their work was over; since obviously their work was over when they died, that settled the discussion. (I never rationalized Sibelius' long final period of non-production; he alone could have done that.) I used to feel fatalistic about man being granted an allotted time to say his piece. (Proof was Poulenc's collapse the morning after he had inscribed the double bar on his last work in progress, answered all letters, and was wondering what to do.)

Today I firmly believe Bill Flanagan died too soon. He left so much undone! True, his last completed work (and by general consensus his best), *Another August*, was finished over two years before his death. But of the many pieces still underway not one will be realized —a pity for a man whose production was already frugal. From that production there is not even a "signature" work identifying him as Copland's *Appalachian Spring* or Barber's *Adagio* identify those composers. Nor did he leave one unflawed song, which could seem ironic given the chiseled, albeit purple, intent of his musical speech, a speech that wanted to say only what needed saying.

But need and speech are separate, especially within an insecure syntax; Bill's conservatory background had not been rigorous enough to allow him the discipline of simplicity. The proper balance that generates a surplus from which an artist draws and learns was for Bill gained through the labor pains of trial and error. I used to kid him about being too smart for prolificity, but he didn't find that funny. He could not practice Forster's motto for creation— speak before you think—but continued to censor, restrain, throttle his muse. The result was a paradoxical fusion of extreme conservatism with extreme unusualness, in effect if not in flavor like Satie.

His critical prose was something else. Though we may never see his presumably near-finished two volumes, on American music and on American theatre, there exists an uncollected mass of published reviews and articles sufficient to fill a sizable book with his special personality: astute, tailored, funny, touching, correct, and wise. He was America's most literate spokesman for the New Right, or the post-avant-garde, a music no longer embarrassed by classical molds or by expressivity as points of departure. These he defended from the inside out, through his dual-natured but enviably modest authority of composer-critic. It is not too much to say he fought a losing battle for his life.

Not even the French can convincingly generalize about the creative process: how artists do, or should, work. For schizoid composers who are also writers, it seems nonetheless obvious that these two vocations satisfy rival drives. Bill's prose was elegant and clear, while his music was turgid and painfully delivered. Half of what he left as completed compositions were, in my opinion, sketches for completed compositions. Still, the other half, along with his prose, comprises tender and truthful treasures, all the more precious for their rarity.

12

Critics Criticized

THE most prevalent literature today is critical analysis; its main subject, the avant-garde. Explications are no longer limited to little magazines but range even to *Vogue.* It is hardly new to state that the New as concept is finished. Yet not only Madison Avenue but "serious" commentators on contemporary culture still throw avant-garde around maintaining that our period is dominated by it. They understand it to mean experimental, yet experiment now is the rule. Everyone is innovating. When self-appointed authority Richard Kostelanetz declares that "an innovative minority makes the leaps that will be adopted by the many," actually the reverse is—always has been—the case: for example, those two monster precursors of The Modern, Wagner and Debussy, were *not* precursors but culminators who stole their seeds from Spohr and Rebikov (nineteenth-century innovators now dismissed) and fertilized them with genius. Or take the Beatles, who in turn took their ideas from the Inventive Many and cohered them into a communicable, and above all, plain art. A great work is so stunningly individual that it strikes us always as new, as a beginning. In fact it is always an end, a point from where we can only start again.

Avant-garde, though implicitly a beginning, now too is an end, an end in itself, an establishment. Hence the impasse. Hence the fancy interpretations of the impasse as vital, when the true vitality long generated by art now probably lies in science. And hence the plight of the conservative composer (himself dismissed as establishment) who lacks a channel for self-defense. He is shoved off the page by interviews with those products of a publicity which, with criticism and rebellion, appear to be The Art of Now.

*

There is something abject about a promoter of the avant-garde. For him the Nowness of a thing is sufficient argument for that thing's favor. Yet that thing, once defined, becomes obsolete, leaving the promoter constantly toeing the crest of the wave or, more correctly, avoiding the blade of his own guillotine.

Conversely, as we should love our neighbor without having to like him, so critics are duty bound to illuminate the Now without having to enjoy it. As a composer, I don't practice this preaching.

Like a writer, a composer despairs of critics who miss the point, not of what he is saying but of how he is saying it. My music is "accused" of simplicity when it is precisely for simplicity I strive. Simplicity can be style, terror-strickenly misread for content. And what certain literary reviewers, in their germanitude, label as "precious" in my verbal *œuvre*, I intend as ironic.

How can one learn, faced with competent contradiction?

From two reviews of *Music & People:*

> "Rorem is worst when refighting his own creative demons, the *Miss Julie* opera that was distressingly received."
>
> —*Kirkus Service*

> ". . . the best thing in it is the detailed, high spirited, and hair-raising account of what it's like to compose and present an opera in America, in this case Rorem's *Miss Julie.*"
>
> —*Alfred Frankenstein*

*

The New York Review of Books, the best literary periodical in America, does not publish musical opinions except (and then but rarely) by Igor Stravinsky and Virgil Thomson. Stravinsky's opinions are couched in interviews, mostly autobiographical. Thomson's are offered as high culture more than common review. One exception: my article on the Beatles, which was doubtless accepted less for its musical than for its sociological information.

As for *Partisan Review*, how have the mighty fallen! Its musical notions are either pretentiously misfocused (Richard Poirier on the Beatles), or inept (Geoffrey Cannon on rock), while its literary criticism now ranges from old-hat false-premise Freudianism (G. S. Rousseau on J. A. Symonds) to who-cares-anymore (Leo Bersani on Henry James).

The New Yorker's recent updating of viewpoint finds them publishing one Anthony Hiss, the first paragraph of whose "in depth" article on Harry Partch, inspired by a new Columbia release, contains a puerile clause worthy of their "Letters We Never Finished Reading" department: ". . . until Columbia brought him to my attention I had never heard of him." Partch, whose recordings for twenty years have been widely available on other than big commercial labels, has always been a substantial name to any curious freshman in American Music.

In *New York* magazine one finds the otherwise sophisticated Alan Rich's compulsion to swing with the times as inadvertently patronizing as: ". . . the audience seemed to know instinctively when [Leon Kirchner's] work was over, which is a tribute both to its perceptiveness and to Kirchner." He grows increasingly apprehensive about liking anything without apologizing for liking it. For instance, he calles me "a composer whom I respect greatly even though his musical leanings are toward a conservative point of view."

His colleague in those pages, John Simon, who usually reviews theater, is careful and spry, necessities for one so consistently hard to please. I do relish that brand of continental bitchery even while it falls tackily back on puns. Simon's only ingenuous proposal (ingenuous, as when non-specialists invade special territory with enthusiasms that come off as harmlessly touching, such enthusiasms having been long ago considered and rejected by specialists) was that musical comedy might be saved by experienced composers like Samuel Barber or, of all people, Elliott Carter. The proposition is inconceivable, assuming that either of these people would want to "save" the musical. Granting the questionable possibility that the genre could be reinforced by a "good" composer, Barber seems a logical choice only to laymen because for them his music sounds lyrical and accessible, and because he is said to prosodize and melodize in manners appealing to concert singers. Now precisely these virtues would keep him from composing something "popular" in the vaster sense. It's hard to be simple, really simple, especially for composers used to dealing with operatic voices. Francis Poulenc, famous for his songs which like Barber's are in the repertory of all "serious" singers, could never (though he often tried) compose convincingly for "the people." But his friend, Georges Auric, a composer whose concert language was not long and flowing and serene, but short and knotty and complex, when turning his talents to pop, hit the jackpot. Because his natural gift was nonmelodic, Auric, when faced with the problem, *fabricated* tunes easy enough for instancy, reducing his toughness to lowest terms. . . . Elliott Carter might thus seem a more logical candidate for musical comedy's salvation, had he not publicly concluded in the 1940's, when he "wrote simply," that no one cared; what he must privately have discovered was that, unlike Auric, his talent for communication was something less than nonmelodic.

What then of the obvious candidate, Leonard Bernstein, on his tightrope between two domains? His concert songs are really show tunes dolled up, his show tunes are concert songs dolled down. Both categories work on their home ground, but are not interchangeable. One cannot imagine Bernstein's show tunes on a standard Town Hall recital (though Eva Gauthier used to insert Gershwin between Gounod and Griffes—one wonders with what effect), but he did write "straight" songs that were convincing in at least *Candide*.

The problem lies partly with performers. Not that Barbra Streisand couldn't handle certain arias if she wished, but her timbre is geared in other directions. By the same token Grace Moore, more recently Eileen Farrell, just never had it when trying to swing. I've yet to hear a vocalist who is adept in both areas.

*

Even the estimable dates quickly when dealing not with art but with art's sociology. Considered today, certain of yesterday's utterances on homosexuality sound ingenuous.

To suggest that "outlets for the work of living American composers are extremely few, which means that homosexual cliquishness could—some informed people say it does—throttle free musical expression," is to ignore that such cliquishness hasn't existed in musical circles, if it ever did, since 1945. In 1945, however, the International Society for Contemporary Music, and the League of Composers, which represented the American composer's chief outlets, were reproached mainly for Jewish cliquishness. Is there one homosexual, composer or otherwise, who today holds a key position for dispensing largesse to new music produced by homosexuals?

To suggest that contact with art "dealing directly with homosexual experience could deepen understanding of aspects of heterosexual relationships" (here, as above, the quotation is from Benjamin DeMott) is to patronize the homosexual artist as one patronizes women or Negroes: a pat on the back, not only for having something to say, but for saying it *as* a homosexual (or a woman or a Negro).

Is there really homosexual art as such, any more than heterosexual (or female or black) art? Art may come from the experience of being these things; but insofar as art restricts its message—indeed, tries for a message at all—it confines itself to propaganda.

*

Nat Hentoff's truculence is embarrassing to any age, when he puts down Howard Nemerov for not knowing Bob Dylan. Seniors can't keep up on *all* their juniors and still get their own work done. Any poet knows the times are a-changing without having to applaud the singer's simplisticisms.

"They don't want your jugular, man," Hentoff righteously informs Pete Hamill about the Rolling Stones, his ear on the same leaden par with theirs. He himself is less engaging than his *engagement*, lacking the charm of his colleague Paul Goodman at his most irksome. Goodman's appeal comes through the vulnerability that is inseparable from creative talent, the best of which is insecure, self-doubting. Hentoff's judgments are often right—I mean left—but expressed without gift.

*

Some spokesmen, like the avant-garde Kostelanetz on
the one hand, or rock critic Richard Goldstein on the
other, set up straw men so as to plug an issue; they are
nevertheless passionate specialists. Some, like Hentoff
or Poirier, while shining brightly in their respective
domains of politics and literature, are simply unin-
formed in matters musical, treating those matters precisely as literature and politics. Others describe those
matters sociologically, peripherally as homosexual—
which is always absorbing. Still others, like Rich and
Simon, describe them within a professional context,
and are a pleasure to read except when treading on toes
too close to home. Of those mentioned, only Stravinsky
and Thomson are practicing musicians; they are also,
perhaps coincidentally, by far the most memorable
writers. But it is no coincidence that, more than the
others, in the realest sense they know what they are
writing about.

Which leaves Joan Peyser, a category in herself—
the critic who by missing the point damns the product
for its chief assets. Let me offer a criticism of her
criticism of a criticism of her criticism:

In the *Sunday Times Book Review* Joan Peyser
reviewed David Amram's autobiography, *Vibrations*.
Maurice Peress challenged her review by a letter in
that paper, which Mrs. Peyser answered, January 12,
1969 [the brackets are mine]:

Maurice Peress, who appears throughout the pages of
this book and is a close friend of Amram's, applies
devastating criteria to his own art. "Loving, tender,

open, sometimes gawky, always his very own" could characterize the creations of many a child.

[—as well as the creations of Schumann, Satie, Ives, Gershwin, and the child all artists must be.]

No one would apply such standards by themselves

[*Who*, no one? Nor are the standards applied by themselves.]

to a new painting, a play or a poem. Why should they serve for the music of our time? I did not review *Vibrations* in order to attack Mr. Peress's friend. I reviewed it to inform

[By what authority?]

the intellectual community, unfortunately estranged from new musical ideas,

[If the intellectual community is estranged from new musical ideas, then why is that community intellectual? (And is *Vibrations* a new idea?) Besides, the intellectual community does not take its cues from the *Sunday Times Book Review*.]

that the author is in a class by himself: neither Amram's glib music nor his chic social style is shared by the serious composer of our day.

[His music is not glib, it is callow. His social style is scarcely chic, it is pseudo-gauche. The chic style, however, applies to Stravinsky, Boulez, Milhaud, Henze, who have the curiosity and wherewithal to seek out good food in the company of the leading minds and personalities of our day.]

How is the reader to know that this is so? Milton Babbitt, Luciano Berio, Lejaren Hiller and their colleagues do not expose themselves through chronicles of their lives.

[But in *Chronicle Of My Life* Stravinsky chronicled his life. Rousseau chronicled his. So did Berlioz, Wagner, Honegger, Antheil, Nicolas Nabokov, Thomson, the Beatles, myself, all to worthy critical acknowledgment.]

A "super-organized musicant" *must* intrude and set the matter straight.

And I must intrude to expose Mrs. Peyser for the interferer that she is, while handing her straight A's for being what Brigid Brophy once called Simone de Beauvoir: a plodder.

And Amram? Admittedly, he is not what the reviewer would term "the serious composer of our day." He is the non-musician's musician. So is Milton Babbitt, on the other side of the same coin. Amram's is a romantic image for lay swingers, Babbitt's is a scholarly image for lay intellectuals, neither category with much musical taste or disposition or real information.

*

Where true vitality is found, criticism seems most superfluous. Unlike the musical scene, movies don't need criticism for nourishment. The brilliant words we read about film are literally exercises in the dark which, from the pens of Pauline Kael or Parker Tyler, themselves become art. Music criticism sparkling on its own (forget about what's being criticized) turns dull and meaningless before what needs dissecting.

13

Twenty Years After

> Look at yourself all
> your life in a mirror
> and you'll see death at
> work like bees in a
> glass hive.
> —JEAN COCTEAU

> When one of us dies,
> I'll move to Paris.
> —PAUL GOODMAN

Japan Airlines (Flight #2, New York to Paris)
29–30 September 1969

Not that I haven't been warned. Logic alone
would indicate that in a country where most of my
friends are a generation older, many should now be
dilapidated. Some may snub me because of *The Paris
Diary*, though surely the French have more urgent concerns than to begrudge me that light book after so
long. But others will not answer phone messages
simply because they're dead.

Around midnight. Airborne in darkness, this novel
choice of transport provides geishas to comply with

133

"passenger needs," while in the next seat by happy coincidence (I being the original hypochondriac) one of my many medical doctors snores a duet with the motor's purr counterpointing my wakefulness. The craft is virtually empty, though by another coincidence we find Sono Osato, whom I've known since childhood in Chicago, with her husband Victor Elmaleh, and chat for an hour over an inedible supper, then retire. The take-off, as usual, was appalling in its rightness, purposeful as an erection, by contrast with the landing, always mundane as death. Here now are suspended hours for thought collecting as the Japanese plane becomes a time machine retreating toward a personal French past.

This brief return to Paris is my first in over five years, the first since reaching my forties, the first since the issue of my four books. For the Parisians, I left as a musician, come back as an author. Five years. But it's been twenty since I went there to live (*earning* the arrival, as anyone does who takes a boat). The ostensible purpose for this twenty-one-day Economy Excursion (ending with a week in England), other than to swallow a healthy draft of the past and then hush for another spell, is to compose an essay whose subject will be a comparison of Then with Now, generally in society and the arts, particularly in the musical scene. Whatever way I am received will be the right way, for as it will nourish my narrative, I can't lose. I declare it self-protectingly, being panic-stricken.

For two weeks I'll have Guy Ferrand's apartment alone in the Rue des Epinettes. Thus my original impulse was to give a mammoth party, mailing invitations before leaving America, seeing who would not come, who would bring new faces, who would no longer be alive. Such Proustian gestures are risky, expensive, vulgar. My present impulse is Dumasian, and the fragility of *Vingt Ans Après*.

Way after midnight, the horizon's aglow. Hurtling toward the future while drunk on the past. Yesterday, in preparation for the "tone," I leafed through old date-books. In 1951, for instance, I note (among reminders like *Buy oranges* or *See dentist* or *Phone Heddy about what happened last night*) a casual mention: *Lunch chez Marie Laure with Giacometti, Balthus, Dora Maar*. I did not then know who these people were, assuming they "were" anyone. Yet if today that seems history, it is no more nor less memorable in retrospect. Lunch with the future-great is not the same as with the now-famous. With the now-famous one remembers because one is *supposed* to remember how really unexceptional, at lunch, they perhaps are, or "are."

But it is not people I have missed and now seek, nor even my own vanished self, so much as smells and temperatures, bakeries and rivers. These touching perfumes of the past become, when mixed with personalities grown atrophied, like fetid dinosaur breath. In a sense, the idea I still retain of France is the one I had before I ever knew that country: a France of Rimbaud, Satie, *Les Faux Monnayeurs*, the young Jean Gabin.

More than the taste, the fragrance of *fine à l'eau* transports me. The taste therefore (the effect) takes me not to France of yesterday but to the irrevocable today. Space is possible in the kitchen. Not time. Why drink? Not, anyway, for time remembered.

If I don't go, maybe It will happen. Maybe It is happening now in Danny's bar, at Casey's, in my own parlor—and I'm not there. But has It, really, ever happened? . . . Yes.

Gravity ages us. After forty our jowls, armpits, tits, and kneecaps sag toward the impatient earth. Lean over a glass table and see yourself as you will be in ten years. Now throw back your head, and see how you once were. Like every living thing always, we are all corpses on parole.

The French at least can see themselves aging. Americans can't. Yet collectively we're no longer adolescent, and individually we're less pretty than our reputation. We are prepared for nothing, certainly not for the embarrassment of growth. Children after summer vacation return, along with the oak-leaf bonfires, nervously to mark change wrought on classmates, a very sudden wonder of nail polish on the girls, and on the boys new pubic hair of first maturity. They turn shyly away —but adults *know*. Except, of course, they don't. Every return at every age brings surprise. Now I turn from the embarrassment of death stamped on the features of everyone I've known. *Les neiges d'antan*, since you're wondering, will be all over those autumn streets of France.

Tomorrow has come. My good doctor rubs his eyes bleary with the nocturnal sun. Sono, over there, stretches one leg straight out like Miss Turnstiles of yore, as she waits for tea. In an hour we'll be landing in the Paris I've thought so hard upon for so many invisible years that I'm sick with joy at what I can't possibly find. In the baggage room my suitcase whispers with two little gold-plated Tiffany snuffboxes, gifts which might be refused by Marie Laure and Nora Auric. (The Aurics have preserved a stony silence since my diaries were published, and Marie Laure's not written since 1967.) Will nobody care that I've come? What of the anonymous letter stating: "All but myself attend you with sharpened knives"? Could it have been appropriate that I chose the fall season, *la rentrée*, at once a rebirth and murder, for my humiliation?

The geishas fuss like gnats. I must comb my new sideburns, pee, finish the croissants, swoon (now is the moment), and wonder if the French taxi strikes are done. There's the city!

Final query: What does it mean when, on a last-minute impulse, you change your flight; then, indeed, the plane you were going to take, crashes—but so does the plane you *do* take?

*

38, Rue des Epinettes, Paris XVII
1 October 1969 (forenoon)

The trip from Orly airport to here covers the whole
city. Unslept, unbathed, and thrilled in an overcoat
beneath the hot and unpolluted yellow sky, I was able
immediately to see it as a telegram. Malraux's high-
pressure hosing of not only monuments but private
buildings was just a trickle when I left in 1964. Now
Paris is a blond. If that's a cliché to the jet set, I quote
Paul Taylor who, when chided for choreographing
Beethoven because it wasn't new, replied, "It's new
to me."

Guy's semiluxury high-rise is located near the Boulevard Bessières, an *extérieur* neighborhood unfamiliar
to most Parisians, and where I am regarded deferen-
tially as a Martian purchasing pears, cheese, frozen
coffee. The apartment, swept neat as a pin by Madame
Rose, transported me in time and space, welcomed me
to those anachronistic bibelots I lived among twenty
summers ago in Morocco, and to a pile of mail containing notably a letter from Claude. *Ned, je n'ai ni
l'envie, ni la curiosité de te revoir. Et je souhaite que le
hasard me fera éviter de te rencontrer. Claude.* ("I have
neither the wish nor the curiosity to see you. And I
hope our paths won't cross by accident.")

A valium, a nap, the day fades. The evening, as
arranged months ago, was to be shared with Robert
Kanters. In the quick-falling dark I crossed Paris
again, this time on foot, the few miles between

Epinettes and Robert's beautiful building, 23 Rue de Beaune, directly across from where I briefly lived, and died of cold, chez Jacques Damase in January of '53.

Robert's four-room lodging is ornamented solely with that most attractive of furnishings, books: on shelves, tables, toilet floor, some ten thousand, each one cut and perused and dusty, their owner grinning out from among them. He has become healthily pot-bellied and elfin, ruddy and aphoristic, fifty-eight, much the same as when we met, if more self-assured, being now a crucial brick in the critical wall which for Paris, more than for New York, separates reading and reader.

My reason for wanting immediately to see Robert Kanters was affectionate gratitude; he was the only one of the French press to defend my diaries; also the first "intellectual" I knew in Paris, having met him in 1949, as I met everyone then, by collapsing at his table and requesting a chartreuse at the Montana bar where he was seated with Fraigneau, Peyrefitte, and Boudot-Lamotte (none of whom would have inherently objected to the presence of what I then represented), a milieu corresponding to David Sachs' in Chicago a decade earlier.

Despite the international *rétrécissement*, one would conclude, judging from Robert (with whom I avoid discussing music, an area in which, like most cultured people, he is lost), that American literature, including *Portnoy's Complaint*, is no more in vogue here than ever. But he asks a few polite questions, mostly about the theatre, that being the domain where writers' names are better known than their writing, at least in the

United States. (France has never produced the sociological equivalent of a Hemingway.) Tennessee Williams and Edward Albee, for example, are certainly more famous than their works, while Myra Breckenridge is surely more famous than Gore Vidal. But where Albee and Williams have *peaked*, as the saying goes, Vidal remains stable, he being also a mind, an *idea* mind; idea men, for better or worse, are more adaptable to changing weather than are poets. Williams and Albee, try though they might, have never produced idea plays like Sartre's or even Giraudoux's; they are sensualists with good ears. They may ultimately be revived or forgotten utterly. Death brought oblivion to Gide and Hindemith, stardom to Bartók and Poulenc. Meanwhile home is represented here by an apparently hideous production of *The Boys in the Band*.

At ten we went to dine on the right bank, again on foot, meaning I have to guide Robert, who is losing his eyesight, over the perilous Carrousel bridge. In my recall, Paris' plan had become a maze: what Avenue led from one *quartier* to another? Once here, the reorientation's so immediate, so exact, I've almost no need to visit old haunts, knowing just where and how they'll be. When, then, at the sudden encounter of an eyesore —Saint-Germain transformed into a circus, Gare Montparnasse a gooey hole like an extracted wisdom tooth— I recoil.

Filets of sole in the bistro of the Rue Sainte Anne. Of course at the next table are Bernard Minoret and entourage exactly as I left them, sleeping beauties gossiping, years ago. Eyes closing from thirty-six

wakeful hours, I made a date with Robert Kanters to
see Alberto Moravia's play on my final French evening
(Monday the 13th), then taxied here and went pro-
foundly to bed.

Now sun streams through the open window. In an
hour I go to 11 Place des Etats-Unis, for lunch at
Marie Laure's.

"Madame la Vicomtesse is a bit behind schedule.
But Monsieur Rorem has only to make himself at
home."

Is this the house I lived in seven years? Like the
streets last night, each corner and every odor here is so
familiar, so utterly the photography of conscious recall
rather than from the maze of dreams, that I feel no
transport: neither admiration at the luxury nor nostalgia at a home regained. I cannot *see* the place, since
I live here yet.

Alone, awaiting the hostess, I nevertheless reinspect
the hexagonal parlor of the ground floor, the most perfectly proportioned and exquisitely appointed single
place on this planet, combing my hair as once I combed
it for two thousand days, in the huge mirror above the
grate where now a small fire burns although the floor-
to-ceiling casements are opened onto the garden whose
late summer breeze hardly stirs the still-green bushes
along the gravel paths, and from over the high granite
walls come the cries of *pétanque* players spending
lunch hour in the Place des Etats-Unis as they have
every noon for decades. There is the pale wood Gaveau
neatly groaning beneath a fortune of marble eggs and
satin art books as before; here stand the same vast vases

heavy with azure chrysanthemums flown in this morning from Charles de Noailles' estate in Grasse; in that
angle the walnut liquor cabinet still stocked with gold
tongs and Perrier water in silver containers; everywhere taste (so much more than *good* taste) gleams:
from amber pillboxes, from the vermeil chinoiseries,
the million-dollar rug like a rose window on the floor,
the smaller masterpieces from the great Noailles col-
lection smiling from the walls of this room which for
the French bourgeoisie has been as often described
(though for opposite reasons) as Mae West's white
Hollywood apartment. The three Goyas have been
removed to the upper stairwell, I noticed on entering,
while passing through with André, the grayer but
always inscrutable *maître d'hôtel*. Otherwise, except for
my face in the mirror, nothing has changed.

Marie Laure will come in, take a wide silent look.
Eh bien, il n'en reste rien, she finally will declare.
"You kept it longer than any of us. Now it's gone,
there's nothing left." And we will go into lunch.

Marie Laure comes in, takes a wide silent look. *Eh
bien, je te trouve très bien*, she declares, settling that
question, so we kiss and are pleased. She herself now
seems benign, looking the same only more so. The
heat's still there, but the fire's out. I am in love with
her. She scares me a little when accepting the disc of
my *Water Music* and the Tiffany trinket with those
raptures of childlike gratitude indigenous to (though
not always demonstrated by) the very rich. The ten-
sion is dissolved by the simultaneous entry of the
Vicomte [Charles de Noailles] from his mother-of-pearl

quarters elsewhere in the fifty-room mansion, and of
Marcel Schneider from the outside world, accompanied
by a bearded Turk who says nary a word for the next
two hours. With which we five adjourn to lunch, not
as formerly in the blue dining room, but in the foyer,
I to be seated at Marie Laure's right, across from
Marcel, behind whom hangs Géricault's painting of
twenty horses' asses to grace my constant view.

The overrich meal is semistylishly served by the
suave but edgy André with an unaccustomed appren-
tice, and as usual the midday sight of red meat seems
repulsive. Like the salad, in seven shades of pale green,
the buttered potatoes are paradisiacal; not so the des-
sert, a *clafoutie* of apples with powdered sugar and a
leather crust. During the ingestion of these I grow
easy, find myself the appraiser.

Charles has undergone a *coup de vieux*, must be
seventy-seven now and looks it, skin powdery, shoul-
ders stooped, verbal intonations pinched (but still so
upper class). One of the world's wealthiest inhabitants,
he remarks, when I ask if he ever visits New York (he
owns half of Wall Street): "I'd love to, but the trip's
so horribly expensive, you know." This, plus the word
"nigger," launched in an English-spoken phrase floating dismally present but unacknowledged like a fart,
raises my eyebrows. Nonetheless I tell him, in full ear-
shot of the servant André who knows family history:
"On the plane yesterday I read Francis Steegmuller's
portrait of Barbette who claims you are—*en toute sim-
plicité*—the one real gentleman left on earth." Applause
from Marcel. Charles feigns interest, but denies knowledge of either Steegmuller or Barbette. Marie Laure

interjects that Steegmuller (whom she's surely mistaken for Frederick Brown) must be that historian who last year asked everyone about Cocteau's genitalia, which she herself now surmises to have been pinkish, crinkly, and capable of ejaculation without friction. From which she proceeds in *non sequitur* to doubtful (if brief) epigrams. Example: "I no longer believe in justice, only in injustice," pointing one finger skyward, as Cocteau used to, signifying bravo. Another example (to make me welcome): "All Americans are children." Has time stopped? Were they, to whom I owe so much, always like this? Was I? Am I? . . . Coffee is announced.

This beverage as usual is provided in the large upstairs parlor to which we now repair (via a new elevator), and there find André preparing a fire. "That's no way to make it burn," barks Marie Laure. "*Mais si, Madame la Vicomtesse,*" he answers back, which he never used to. "No, it isn't." The exchange occasions my sinking into this protective enclosure I so loved, to constitute what has and hasn't budged. The huge portraits, by Balthus and Bérard and Berman, of Marie Laure, have been stored out of sight because, I suppose, she avoids reminders of youth. Unchanged, however, among the Rubenses and Dalis, is the upholstery which everywhere needs repair, and the white ceiling, thirty feet up there, still brown with water stains.

An examination of Marie Laure's own recent painting reveals her personal celestial domain intact, with feathery fingers beckoning us to jump right into the canvas and join her there among her edible colors. I make a date for next Tuesday with Marcel (he being one of the critics I want to interview), make a date for tonight with Marie Laure (she wanting me to meet Pietro Clementi), and, somewhat dazed, come back here where at 5 o'clock I'm expecting Jacques Bourgeois.

Jacques looked marvelous in a new toupee, subtly gray and seemingly expensive. On telling him I'd just seen Marie Laure, he answered, "I decided to accept lunch at Marie Laure's again about three years ago: same guests, same conversation, as three years previous." He doesn't remember that in 1964 I asked him if he still saw Marie Laure, and he replied, "Well, I went to lunch again a few years back: same conversation, same guests as always."

He continues: "If I look well, it's because, as Maurice Béjart says—and it's Béjart above all (along with Maria—Maria Callas) whom I promote these days, now that I'm a freelance broadcaster—he says 'There are two kinds of people, the young and the old, and it has nothing to do with age.' You and I, Ned, are young. And most certainly so is Béjart, it stems from his originality, despite your feeling he's the poor man's Robbins. . . . How can I realize if things have changed in Paris? except, naturally, that most of the people are dead, or act like it. Music-wise it's become a sort of avant-garde capital: Varèse is the classical master, and the most popular American is John Cage. There's a whole new public of enthusiasts who worship the trinity, Xenakis, Stockhausen, Berio, while utterly ignoring Mozart symphonies. . . . Jolivet? No place left for him. No room for 'La Jeune France,' for those intermediaries like Jolivet and Dutilleux and Daniel Lesur. Messiaen *is* grudgingly acknowledged as a tiresome grandfather."

He adjusts his custom-made beige leather trousers, sips at his nonalcoholic drink, finishes the pear tart, and brings forth a Polaroid color snapshot of "the young friend," a painter posed before his easel which sustains a trashy portrait of Jacques himself. "This is our *jeunesse*. France now has a public, a great big knowledgeable young public for ultramodern art."

"Like America's for rock?"

Jacques is unsure. But he is anxious to impress the fact that the Events of May, 1968—*les événements*— were a liberation for more than just civil rights. "And Karajan, *mon cher*, is *the* big *moment musicale* here: his three concerts next week have been sold out for over six months."

"But what about Xenakis?" I asked, confused by the sudden catholicity.

"It was I who first brought him to the radio, who first understood, intellectually, his music, rather than just bathing in it. I swear it makes a difference to know where he's aiming, to study assiduously, as I have, his stochastic method. And what more can I say than that with this method he creates an environment, a land, that doesn't bore me to visit?" With which he stood up, having a date with the young friend, and I one with Marie Laure. At my request he revealed the French name for mineral oil *(huile de paraffine)*, since traveling gives me problems. Then he left.

Not a word about my work. Jacques Bourgeois, forty-seven, music critic, knows that to age is not to flow gently, but to jerk from plateau to plateau, mostly downward; hence the jitters of reunions, the need to show his up-to-dateness despite (have I noticed them?) those crows' feet 'round his twinkling eyes. What with Béjart and Callas he is well-rounded, I suppose, as music critics ought to be. But to hop on the artistic bandwagon of the young is to lose your identity, Nazi style. Youth as mass may be correct politically, never artistically: how to write music is not a mass decision.

Confronted by the cold fact that I'm no longer a potential, but an accomplishment—that I *have become*—means both terror and strength. Jacques' rôle is to be open-minded. Mine isn't.

At 8:30 fetched Marie Laure who meanwhile had been to the hairdresser, and was now impatiently waiting in her lobby, befurred and with bangs cute as Betty Boop's, leaning against César's ten-ton sculpture of a smashed automobile. She took me uninvited to Dino di Meyo's. Clementi never showed up, so we dined *à trois* on poached eggs and fish and a kind of chocolate paste at a minuscule table overhung with palms. Strictly gossip, mostly about Raffaello de Banfield's première this Friday, and about Louise de Vilmorin who is (as everyone but me knows) Malraux' mistress, but losing interest rapidly now that Malraux no longer, etc. Then to my stupefaction Dino turned on the television and Marie Laure, enthralled, consumed a 1942 war movie from start to end. French TV does have the saving grace of clarity compared to ours, with sixty rather than forty lines per inch, or something like that.

We all drive back to the Place des Etats-Unis, where, until midnight, we examine ML's scrapbooks containing mostly details on the 1968 *événements*. But I am too weary to concentrate on the dizzy talk accompanying each image. The fragrance of fire and fresh fruit becomes almost painful, so I excuse myself, thereby concluding my first full day back in Paris.

*

Thursday, 2 October
Cold and sunny. Fitful night.

Jacques Bourgeois' magnanimous points of view kept me awake. A composer can't afford to be magnanimous except about himself. Audiences may be dumb; but from a theatrical (if not a musical) standpoint, so is the avant-garde. The public will rather quickly grasp a theatrical (if not a musical) point, while composers just plod on. Eric Salzman, for instance. As to stochasticism, only secondarily do I care how a piece is made. First I must care about the piece. Seams show in any masterpiece, of course, for beauty limps—that's *The Blood of a Poet*. Babbitt's total order and Cage's dice are fine, but their results are all seams, seams in space, as it were, minus the whole cloth. Art is a retention of childhood, not a return to childhood. Cage's "environmental" *Tunnel of Love* is a return, an expensive return, while Babbitt has no childhood at all. He's quite grown up.

At *16 heures*, a visit to Didier Duclos, new director of my music publisher Boosey & Hawkes' continental office. As contrasted to his predecessor, the suavely

handsome Mario Bois, Duclos is bespectacled (like me)
and eager, with that eagerness of agony: enthusiasm
for lost causes. Presumably my visit is promotional,
but like yesterday there now come the praises of
Xenakis who is not only the current French hero, but
Boosey & Hawkes' chief product—after Stravinsky—
of export. (As an American, I'm a product of import,
without importance.) Again, like yesterday, I ask if
the local lust for this composer corresponds to our
young freaks' for rock. Again, no clear answer. Or
don't the French know that rock is meant to be a Way
of Life? Can it be that their avant-garde is "appreci-
ated" by such gigantic numbers on strictly musical
terms? The young, the blacks, can, after all, be stupid
like most people; still, to direct mass ignorance toward
something essentially intelligent (and abstractly intelligent at that, which our rock isn't) seems both bizarre
and old-fashioned, the avant-garde being in France a
1920's impulse, theoretically repugnant to revolution-
aries.

Thoroughly cordial, with token encouragement about
getting performances, Didier Duclos promises to phone
next week, hands me some pamphlets on Xenakis, and
says good-bye.

From Boosey & Hawkes' office in the Rue Druout,
I walk to Boulevard de Clichy where I am to drink tea
with the Milhauds. The intervening labyrinth of grad-
ually mounting streets and seething grocery stores
which reopen at sunset when everyone's going home,
of the communist headquarters at Chateaudun, of
Notre Dame de Lorette, and especially the Rue Pigalle,

revives another promenade, that one nocturnal, in these byways eighteen years ago with George Chavchavadze who, like everyone else musical then, was selling me to the city and the city to me. We were ensconced, George every inch the Russian prince with his gold toothpick, I with bleached hair and nine-foot scarf a-trailing, at a bar in the Place Blanche, when a black-haired Legionnaire offered us five thousand francs if I would, for the next half-hour, croon Kentucky lullabies to him in a room of the nearby Hôtel des Martyrs. Did I? I remember only the following summer in their Venetian palazzo, Princess Elizabeth Chavchavadze in her eyeglasses, still very fat, working at petit-point while George gave a lesson to Philippe Entremont on the nuances of Liszt. Soon after came Elizabeth's Swiss sleeping cure from which she emerged slender and self-assured with new conversation, but the same pair of glasses. Then their death together, gratuitous and sharp, when their car fell over a cliff, poignantly relieving earth—as does all death, I suppose—of the last representatives of a certain life style. The style was promoted less by money (there's still plenty of that around) than by conjoining of art with high society at the expense of political involvement, a conjoining exemplified at its height by Diagheleff (to whom war was an inconvenience, as indeed, in its realist sense, war always is for artists, because when war imposes itself as subject matter it turns more urgent than the art it impels, which in turn turns to propaganda), at its decline by Edith and Etienne de Beaumont (whom I, perhaps luckily, certainly historically, visited with Marie Laure in 1951, shortly before their respective deaths from natural causes, and was properly subdued by their urban castle, still standing behind its white wall at 2 Rue du Roc, decorated with maquettes of *Tricorne* and *Parade*, ballets originally financed by Etienne, a lovable Charlus), and at its corrupt collapse, confiscated in America by the Sculls, the Hornicks, and their likes.

I am the only guest at the Milhauds. They appear weary, having arrived this morning from England, though Darius in particular looks healthier than when we last met two years ago in Oakland. Having been summoned for tea, tea is indeed served, plus a heap of absolutely juicy cookies baked expressly by Madeleine for the occasion, or so she says. They are unleavened, oatmealy, and brushed before cooking with a faint film of peach. I ate fourteen.

Tactfully and without insistence Madeleine incessantly talks, speaking for two, like a pregnant woman, filling the lacunae of Darius who nods sometimes painfully. Like her voice, her fingers constantly move, around the knitting in her lap, while she weaves the mutual verbs of our gossip forever to where her husband can easily interject his intelligence. Last night in London they sat through Colin Davis' uncut version of *Les Troyens*, found it sublime. Such an admission seems more foreign to me than the Milhauds themselves seemed twenty years ago. This late afternoon we all felt like Americans in Paris, momentarily immune to native darts.

The rush hour of Paris being every bit the joke it's reputed to be, my taxi needs seventy minutes from Place Clichy to the Eiffel Tower. During the trip my traveling companion, touch-and-go colitis, reappears with renewed vigor. At my destination on the Elisée-Reclus resides Adrien Perquel, once jealously described by Marie Laure (who has never met him) as my one *mauvaise fréquentation*, but who is really a luxuriantly successful Jewish banker of seventy-three, met on the Ile-de-France in 1952, a ladies' man, and a faithful acquaintance with whom it is thrilling to realize I have no friends in common.

For years I languish about a given corner of this city, find it again and die. Then once the fact of being here is established—a question of an hour—the geography of memory falls into place. Thus there's no reason to rush back to first homes, in the Rue de la Harpe, and shed tears. I know they're there, urban proportions being safely reinstated, and like vital shots of whiskey they can wait, isolated on altars, maybe even improving with age.

And so it is tonight tête à tête with Adrien. I have consumed this identical meal a hundred times, admired these too-marvelous manners before, attended each vicarious question ("Why is America so pornography-minded? so much more so than France?"), examined every so-so Kisling, and telescoped the costly fibrous lineaments that hold my host's toupee in place (do all the French wear them now?). What's new? What have we else? Paul Goodman's verses come to mind:

> . . . It is impossible
> to live with birds and beasts as if they were like us.
> If I do not associate with people
> with whom shall I associate?

152

After supper the colitis has not eased. Which isn't why I decline Perquel's liqueurs: for eighteen months I've scarcely touched alcohol or tobacco, reasons of health and work and domesticity.

That voice, always interrogative, obliges me to reorder the conversation, since I'm still unrecovered from Monday's flight. "You all keep talking about *les événements*, those May Events, as though they combined the French Revolution with the Second Coming. Define them." The May Events: a fatal juggling of authority, a never-to-be-gone-back-on reassessment of who's boss in any relationship, parent and child, student and teacher, employer and employee, subject and state, even artist and critic.

The present tone of Paris—at least as I've heard it up to now—sounds removed from our Vietnam, which the French compare to their Algeria. No one talks of Nixon, and fantastically I feel safe, as though tomorrow the horrors would sail from China, high over France, and land with a terminal crash in faraway New York.

Bored by the same tune, yesterday from Marie Laure and tonight from Perquel, describing Americans as children. The French clutch at this faded notion which excites them the way southern white housewives are said to be excited by Negro janitors. In fact, our degeneration into adolescence resulted precisely in 1957 from the simultaneous shock of Sputnik and Little Rock; our ensuing decay into adulthood appeared with this year's reaction to our new president; we seem headed as fast as Europe toward senility. In answering my own questions I learn little new about the country where I'm now a guest, unless it's that I push things to my own conclusion.

Preparing to leave Perquel I examine carefully his entire house, its boatlike structure, the downstairs kitchen, immense ceilings and long rooms, garden, gymnasium, Chinese relics everywhere, the best painters' worst paintings, and a carpet you really do sink into. Because I'll probably never be there again.

2 A.M. I've been reading *Le Figaro Littéraire* and the Xenakis literature. The former contains an amusing (to an American) poll organized by Claude Rostand, which asks various notables how they feel about a *stranger*, Herbert von Karajan, coming to be the conductor of the newly organized Orchestre de Paris. This inversion of American viewpoint follows an article, "in depth," on the movie *More;* a report of the near-obligatory suicide of the Marseille school mistress of thirty who was sleeping with one of her students, and Pompidou's summation of *cette tragédie* in a quote of Eluard; the wise and boring Bloc Notes of the unkillable Mauriac.

As for the Xenakis, should go to bed, stomachache, tomorrow will be huge, but just a word, before stale ideas grow staler:

". . . *le jeu facile*, the nondifficult manner belongs to an esthetic and to a musical conception which are no longer timely. Because we've changed our perception, our way of thinking and of doing."

No. We have grown not more but less difficult. Look around, at what makes a difference, and at what doesn't.

". . . *de nos jours*, it takes a lot to be shocking, because we expect everything and we believe everything."

And we believe nothing.

". . . *Dans ma musique* there is all the anguish of my youth, of the resistance. . . . The traditional expressions of sensibility change as fast as dress design. . . . What's important in today's music is its abstract nature."

Importance is not the qualifier of "abstract nature" in today's music, since the nature of all music of all times has been abstract. The preceding remark is worthy of Casals, a remark which contains its own destruction, and accordingly that of composer Xenakis himself. Regarding the anguish of his youth, that is hardly abstract, yet forms the basis of his creativity.

". . . *Enfin*, the interest is to create a form of composition which is no longer the object in itself but an idea in itself."

Well, that is one interest. His premise is arbitrary: that inspiration is a thing of the past; nor can he prove that his own work is not inspired exactly as inspiration was defined in the good old days.

But I've not read far into this interview. These are quick reactions.

*

Sunday afternoon, 5 October

Such perfect weather more than any person breaks the heart since beauty always wounds, but Adrien Perquel the other night talked of his "mediocrity" and coming death as he did twelve years ago, though now he's seventy-three. I've bought a large plum pie, some Scotch, and eight plump ruby roses, for at sundown Maxine Groffsky's coming over, and also: Robert Veyron-Lacroix, Jean-Michel Damase, Jean Chalon, Jean De Rigault, Henri [José] Hell, and maybe Raffaello de Banfield. The flowers: because here I don't seem, yet, to have hay fever.

The evening of last Friday was to signify my trial by fire. That morning as usual I ingested hot croissants with icy butter and foamy *café au lait*, seated at the kitchen window, watching the frenzy of the street. Friday being market day in the *quartier*, the block is blocked off, double lines of provisional canvas kiosks are erected, manned by women (. . . *des femmes à grosses poitrines/Et bêtes comme chou* . . .) hawking their pure gold squash and healthy yellow tomatoes compared to which ours look like garbage.

I made a note about feeling lost and sad, though today, feeling well (such perfect weather more than any person, etc.), how stretch that out beyond declaring I felt lost and sad? Phone call from PQ in Marseille inviting me down, a voice unheard in years yet familiar as this coffee giving rise to dreams until another call, from Marie Laure, explicated: "Some say you mistreated me. But tonight, we will protect you." The mistreatment referred to the diary; she had nonetheless granted written permission to quote letters, and to say anything except about her family, and about . . . [another provision]. Bargain kept. Her "we" referred to herself and Dino. "Tonight" meant the triple bill of little operas, by Henri Sauguet, Raffaello, and Manuel Rosenthal, scheduled for observation, Opéra Comique, before a "gala" audience consisting largely of those who used to be my friends.

A third phone call, from myself to Gavoty, revealed that *"Monsieur est dans sa salle de bains,"* which cheered me up. "Would you call back in a quarter-hour?"

N'est pas antitraditionnel qui veut—it's not that easy to slough off the past. Complete in Indian regalia, in front of Sacré Coeur, two French hippie friends meet. And shake hands.

The elite tone of Paris is hardly pseudo-hippie or post-mod like Manhattan's. French Youth, now more appetizing (while French cooking has become less appetizing) than ours, still wears neckties. To be daring is to sport a turtleneck at the theatre, as did my evening companion, Jean De Rigault, although I, forewarned by Sauguet of the evening's sobriety, felt compelled to buy, Friday on the awful Avenue Saint Ouen, black clothes which are now an encumbrance.

No one in that ugly lobby had aged any more than lodgers age in the Grévin Museum. There, instantly, was Claude, naturally with Charlotte Aillaud, leaving me thoroughly indifferent and mildly amused, my *De Profundis* suddenly acquiring a retrospect no more grave than *Lady Windermere's Fan*. Physical pain, unlike moral pleasure, is impossible to reconstruct *en souvenir*. As recommended, I did not say hello.

But I nevertheless tripped over that pair of beauties,

Oh! Jeanne Ritcher, looking so tall and so well pos-
tured beside Nora Auric, the latter still with stars in
her clipped white hair, prettier than Joan of Arc in a
snowstorm. I kissed Jeanne as Nora said *Bonjour monsieur*, then, double-taking, clasped me. *Mais je ne
t'avais pas reconnu!* She melted, and I succumbed to
the prodigal son's relief, and the *entr'acte* turned enjoyable. The surface cruelty of Parisians is gymnastic,
rhetorical push-ups veiling a magnanimity we could
well envy. The bickering feud, the witty censure, justi-
fied or not, are resolved with a "Come home, all is
forgiven." Or so was the implication from greetings of
Jacques Février (who had resented the impudence of
my "the French don't know how to play their own
music"), of the Rostands, of Nora's sister the anesthe-
tist Nadia Dubonnet who quickly collared me about
drugs in the USA, while Marie Laure, in black, stood
over there with a dark young painter, among the pil-
lars, looking curiously absent, but no more curiously
than nineteen years ago.

If socially the early evening thrived, musically it
brought catastrophe. To the social-minded, a definition
for Concert is: that which surrounds an intermission.
Friday was an unflawed example. The operas were
particularly appalling in that I had been so recently
brainwashed about the French avant-garde. Sauguet's
1930's bonbon, *La Gageure imprévue*, mounted (without sets) rather more charmingly two years ago by the
Met Opera Studio, here came off as old-hat oom-pa-pa
and overlong, although with a marvelously simple
décor of a slightly lopsided sea-green eighteenth-cen-
tury interior which Jacques Dupont always manages

with skill. Rosenthal's revival, also from the 1930's, came off as plain uncomfortable with its worn-out Javas and American pratfalls. Dear Raffaello's première, a pastiche of the 1930's and a solo vehicle for Denise Scharley, came off as a tango trying for macabre camp, but missing the boat, as an Italian in this area must. Was the hall blushing? It was not. *Le tout Paris*, no more discriminatory than ever in matters aural, nevertheless murmured later: "If only you had been here last summer when we presented Ives at. . . . If only you could be here next month when we're having Berio at. . . ."

But I am here now.

Supper at midnight with José Hell, Richard Négroux, Jean De R. and his young friend, my first cigarette in two months, first *vin rouge* in two years despite the colitis (which diminished), a round of noisy gay bars, and a drily proud dissertation from Jean De R. on how Youth—capitalized in the Gallic psyche as in the Yankee—doesn't attend such operas, considers Marie Laure, even de Gaulle, as a dinosaur, says *merde* to every form of the past, is not oriented to rock but to the "integrity" of Xenakis, politics, and to. . . . Then he described—and he thinks of himself as Young —how his very old mother (surely a "form of the past") last year died in his arms, leaving him bereft, shattered.

Last night, Saturday, a long duck dinner *chez* José [Henri Hell] with Richard, and gallons of Evian water to assuage a dehydrating hangover. The apartment is directly above Robert Kanters', though it might as well be another world for the resemblance, Robert's being clean disorder, José's the reverse. Richard Négroux, still handsome at fifty and speaking better French than the French but with that rippled accent Rumanian refugees never shed, is José's friend, Dubuffet's secretary, a reader for Fayard, cultured and unpretentious, dapper and without a cent, and without an American equivalent, being descended from the wit of Kafka, a wit as different from our's as two blood types, despite how hard we try to interpret our desperate bureaucracy as central European.

After gruyère and pears, a long long long and languid stroll, covering that multitude of acres which once had been so personal to us three. Boulevard Saint-Germain now filled with dress shops like Saint Tropez, Rue Dauphine seething with apple-cheeked students very conscious of being apple-cheeked students, whose parents, my colleagues, were pale and shorter and under the surveillance of Hitler Youth. Our Rue de la Harpe has become a casbah, albeit a lavishly fake one, there being a visible lack of Algerians in the city since the war's end. Number 53, the scene of my virginity with Xénia, is a movie house showing Bergman's *Le Silence.* At the pastry shop next door we purchase, at one franc each, some rosy-orange Turkish delights, which the French call *loukoums,* speckling ourselves with powdered sugar. By way of Saint Julien des Pauvres we arrive to inspect Notre Dame, hosed clean, itself resembling a *loukoum,* mousebitten and filled with Day-Glo. Health improved, less depressed, incredibly gentle clean Indian summer. At 1 A.M., as a brief warm rain began, my friends put me into a taxi, after accepting an invitation to come by for tea and crumpets this afternoon.

*

Monday morning, 6 October

Since Maxine Groffsky has the best figure in Paris, and means to keep it, she starves herself faint, works out at dance classes, takes sweat baths and (it's rumored) milk baths. Thus she was understandably anguished at the four varieties of salted nuts, not to mention the plum tart with clotted cream, on view at my tea party yesterday. She arrived early and departed eighty minutes later, again understandably, when the *garçons* began to arrive. She accepted two Scotches, consumed a quarter-kilo of almonds with angry despair, tossed back her very long mulberry silk hair every three minutes (it's arranged, like Veronica Lake's, to fall in her eyes), and occasionally walked wonderfully across Guy's narrow Moroccan parlor in the manner a man would like to be turned into a woman in order to emulate. She has just moved from an apartment in the Rue du Dragon (ironically, the address of Charlotte Aillaud whom she resembles like a twin) to an apartment in the Rue de Tournon. Why does she stay on in Paris? Because she needs the higher intelligence ratio, appreciates the responsibility of representing *The Paris Review*, likes her social life, especially Harry Mathews, and feels safer than in America. Next question? Close your eyes and hear the voice, through hers, of Frank O'Hara and all his friends. She had parked her

161

car during a bewilderingly blinding sunset in the near-by but equally bewildering Cité des Fleurs, but as it was dark when she left she got lost, perhaps forever.

The boys, minus Raffaello, chatted for two hours. Then we went to dine *en bande* near the *Odéon* at a bistro sympathetically renovated in *fin de siècle* blood-colored plush.

[A self-addressed memo here suggests depicting each of the boys in relation to their careers, to each other, to my own history, to the state of music, to friendship. But I'm out of practice for diaries, maybe forever. These pages—which I confess are pasted together from reconstructed notes—are so cold yet so unpared, so self-conscious, so endless yet so unrevealing—at least of other people. Who are the other people to be portrayed as loved ones? Only generalities and my ego seem feasible; yet I do require them, those friends, deeply, don't I?

Let me continue nonetheless, more telegraphically, out of a need for order; indeed, to fill an order. *J'ai dit que tout était en ordre*—was the Cocteau curtain line. Intimation: when I soon leave France, everyone will continue in orderly fashion as though I'd wound the clock. Then some urge (for perfection?) will force me to throw away the key. The country will run down. I will never come back. It's excruciating.]

After midnight.

The good-looking—if less so than five years ago—Mario Bois, married to ballerina Clare Motte and formerly with Boosey & Hawkes, now runs a business for himself. For two hours this afternoon he, so very *gentil*, all but beguiled me into a respect for his complex scheme of renting unpublished music by living composers, while retaining a huge percentage of the gross income. He is the third person in three days to announce himself the personal inventor of the great Xenakis. As though I cared—more than for the dry chestnut leaves strewing the Tuileries where I strayed, killing time, before fetching Michel Girard, Rue de Varenne.

Bookstores, errands, *flâneries*, no thought of cruising, only of the gentle city which now that I'm here, what's the difference, neither of us cares, so be passive utterly to the beauty, see all, not with new but with old eyes finally unburdened with ambition.

At nineteen o'clock, October nightfall, jammed streets of hurriers home, you look into windows of expensive restaurants, rue de Grenelle or on the quais, and see a single table crowded with the personnel eating before the first customers appear, and standing around in the emptiness the white waiters wait.

The *rez de chaussée* of Michel Girard and Jean Pétain is no less sumptuous, if somewhat more charged with rarities, than a hundred and twenty months ago. Young skinny whippets replace the old Wagnerian dachshunds on the divans of iodine-green velvet. The heads of the house, taller than ever, gray and nervous, look handsomely haunted and aristocratic after the simulated American-style immediacy of Mario Bois.

In a hired cab Michel escorts me to the excellent

restaurant of my old Hôtel Bisson where, over a *turbot* and coffee, and under the sad stare of my host, I answer his barrage of questions, and he mine. With the deaths of the terribly alive Denise Bourdet, and of Julius Katchen who first introduced us, Michel and I sink into those commiserative bromides that soothe the soul and renew the past. The past when I, a Fulbright Fellow, used to come daily to work at his Pleyel.

The dead. Young Marion Jeanson (but was she young?) with whom one sunny noon I walked the five kilometers from the rue Foyatier, where Monsieur Vadot the copyist lived, to this very Hôtel Bisson where I then lived, without either of us shutting up except for sips of pernod en route. And Valentine Hugo. And Hervé Dugardin, who yesterday in 1951 spoke of Kay Francis as though it were yesterday, but will plainly never speak of her again. Nor will Guy de Lesseps whose dying decapitates a third of the tripartite Medusa which was Auric, for if Georges was Nora's brain, Guy was her brawn, and now she's smarter, but walks, they say, with a limp. Most precious of all, Julius, and our Denise to whom I can't apologize for what she found as *mauvais goût* in the journal. Maybe we'll feel better when we're dead, but that will be the day! Yes, I have been warned—like the little girl in *Our Town*.

But I explain that I've come to Paris less to open coffins than to ease birth pangs, notably those of our mutual acquaintance Gérard Souzay who next month in Philharmonic Hall will introduce my cycle *War Scenes*. He had written last May asking me to provide something new for his November recital and ensuing

American tour. He wanted "dramatic" songs, his voice having grown more "interesting" than before. I fulfilled the commission in ten days, composing to five fevered extracts torn pellmell from Walt Whitman's war journal. Since, *en principe*, I never want to set the French language to music again (it sabotages my inner nature), the choice of Whitman's depressing text served two functions: the words, being a century old, automatically contain archaicisms which won't sound strange on Souzay's tongue, as would the poetry of, say, John Ashbery; and those words are otherwise timely, being vital descriptions of battle: the gore and poignance, ferocious anxiety and placid passion, are as close to Vietnam as to the Civil War. Dalton Baldwin, Gérard's impeccable pianist, had in fact phoned this morning to confirm our Sunday rehearsal date, and to say how much he enjoyed working on the accompaniment, adding, with a shocking naïveté which somehow only an American could pull off, "Thank God the war is still on!"

Michel asks after Marie Laure, not with the snide reference of yore—*et ta logeuse!*—but kindly, with an implication I'm convinced is valid: we grow old without inner change: if we are "good" at twenty we will be good at ninety, but whoever is graceless at ninety (like Somerset Maugham or Marya Freund) was always graceless.

While paying the bill he remarks on my ever-fluent French; and as we emerge into the green night of the Quai des Grands Augustins, he mentions having seen my recent squib *On Nudity* translated in *Carrefour* by Claude Roy. The weather being propitious, we amble to the Louvre to examine the new moats, then to the sand-colored Institut by way of the Bridge of the Arts, and next door La Monnaie, an edifice whose perfection I (nor anyone else) had never noticed before the purges. We said good-night at the corner of the Rue des Saints-Pères, since I had a date to see the film about Rubinstein.

Michel has promised to phone tomorrow after arranging with Julien Green and Robert de Saint Jean (whom, stupefyingly, he's not seen since our evening together in May of 1951) for us all to dine together. But he won't, and we won't.

François Reichenbach's movie on Rubinstein, appropriately called *L'Amour de la vie*, is a most satisfying one-man show, similar to the documentary Reichenbach showed us ten years ago about a black boxer. His not-unknown experiments with pornography have benefited him here, detail and obsession no longer being the telescope of sex but of musical sound. To hear—I mean, to *see*—Rubinstein play Chopin and Schumann, the French line up for blocks at the five cinémas where the film, in crushing color, is distributed.

*

Tuesday, 7 October

The French: talk.

They talk and talk. But not of politics nor of the world's end. At least not to me. Which is fine, since I'm less at home in politics than in art, being less con-

cerned with a country's well-being than with my own
well-being within that country.

Since 1944 I have composed an hour's worth of
music every twelve months. The average was higher
during the early years when impulse gushed without
censorship, lower in later years when discipline presumably played a part, plus the interminable chore of
orchestration which does not add hours to one's total
œuvre, but simply subtracts them from one's life.

The most fruitful single period—though much of the
crop was underripe—came in Morocco between 1949
and 1951 when I wrote my first of everything in the big
forms: quartet, sonata, symphony, opera, song cycle,
concerto. All these are dated in Fez or Marrakech, and
are directly due to the hospitality of Guy Ferrand.

The next most prolific period—though much of the
fruit now seems rotten—came in France between 1951
and 1957 when I composed my second of everything.
All are dated in Paris or Hyères, and are due directly
to the hospitality of Marie Laure de Noailles.

These productive seasons were of protected isolation.
Since then, too, I've worked best in the rural hothouse
confines of self-exile, as at Yaddo or the MacDowell
Colony. The quality result is something else. Some of
my best pieces were simultaneous with (if not the issue
of) a quite hysterical urban renewal. Of the total
twenty-six hours I now qualifiedly claim ten, am not
ashamed of five, and am proud of less than one.

Over the phone the famous voice of Lise Deharme
huskily declares: *Tu es une âme pure, mon chéri, et*

dans Paris il n'y a que deux âmes pures, la tienne et la mienne. Amusing, because Lise surely strikes few people as a "pure soul"; indeed, her most telling trait is a compulsive knack for donning the threadbare cloak of worldliness with an actress' catty grace. Her very books show that she conspires with the devil, not with saints. So I invite her to the little welcome-home party Robert Veyron-Lacroix plans for me tomorrow.

This afternoon, lunch at Nora Auric's. (*Merlan frits*, new potatoes, green salad, *yaourt aux mirabelles*, Spanish coffee.) Within four minutes the corny but comfortable rapport was reestablished: despite absence or misunderstanding we will be close forever. The Tiffany trinket, accepted with relish, did bring forth *"C'est le sentiment qui compte,"* though I'd thought it rather generous.

Surrounded by chrysanthemums in the spacious new apartment, 36 Avenue Matignon, Nora remains pretty beyond belief, but older around the lips, and still protesting about her lack of concern with Marie Laure. We talked until five, mostly of Guy de Lesseps whose agony she recounted (for the first time, apparently) in pungent detail. Since his death she has not spent a night without dreaming of his face, a ruined face, on the hospital pillow. Her too few recent paintings depart radically from the children's portraits and submarine landscapes of the fifties; these are dazzling yellow, a yellow not of optimism but of jaundice.

Georges, due back Friday from New York, also leads an enforced new life, having just turned seventy and become disengaged as director of the Opéra. But he still struggles with the same "creative block," it would seem, since I asked Nora whatever became of the project of a libretto from Simenon. (At curtain rise a girl, standing on the bridge of the Canal Saint Martin, sings an aria, then jumps in the water and drowns.) She shook her head. Then, out of the blue, revived an idea I had proposed ages ago: of making a suite from Georges' scores for *Sang d'un Poète*, *Le Million*, and *Les Jeux sont faits*. But she added sadly, "Oh, it probably wouldn't have worked."

5:30, tea with Marcel Schneider, Rue de Turenne, in that ghostly section of the Left Bank called Le Marais. Mounting the four flights to Marcel's apartment I am reminded of Denise Bourdet's aromatic paragraph about mounting the same four winding flights—a three-sentence evocation of the neighborhood's medieval history, the history of the becloved orange she was carrying as gift to her host, and of the host himself, Marcel, in pristine style, overlooking the Place des Vosges and the Carnavalet. My own gift is a record of Beverly Wolff singing *Poems of Love and the Rain*. Thereupon Marcel immediately inscribes a copy of his new *Guerrier de pierre*.

The purpose for this visit, other than friendliness, is to settle the local state of music. However, by now so many people have told me the same things (their proud avant-garde is firmly and expensively esconced, they love it, or hate it, while defining it as America did around seven years ago: electronic-serial-chance, quite isolated from our current Vulgar-As-Deep, suspicious-of-excellence, syndrome), that my interest lies more in

169

his definition of *Les événements*. When I praise the rose-colored sugar biscuits served with the jasmine infusion, Marcel chortles: *Ca n'a aucun rapport avec des événements*, which he then classifies as Sartre being out, Lévi-Strauss in, or one aristocracy replacing another.

A faintly acrid fragrance issued from somewhere, perhaps from, I might suspect (were he not so fastidious), my host's besandaled feet, or from the early bonfires that are beginning to glow in this most sanitary of cities. Regina Sarfaty phoned to cancel our evening's engagement, leaving me at loose ends, for I was of no mind to accompany Marcel to Andre Watts' recital.

I therefore dined alone on fried eggs at the Flore (reassured by the presence of the unchanged waiters, like the cashier at Loew's Sheridan who, decade after decade, shoots out tickets with flintfaced fidelity), walked to the Etoile, saw (part of) a terrible movie, *L'Américain*, with both Trintignant and Signoret walking through their turgid roles, picked up some magazines at Le Drugstore (France's giddy imitation of nothing ever seen before), and came home.

*

Wednesday, 8 October
Very late at night.

Paris cab drivers. Their masculinity still seems more natural, more earthy (dirty), than ours. Tough. Tough too's their femininity. One of them at four this afternoon deposited me at the Alliance Française where Jean Marais is directing Cocteau's *Oedipe Roi* which he's also doing sets for and starring in. He didn't halt the rehearsal at my arrival; he simply introduced me to everyone, including two puzzled actors on stage. We proceeded to reminisce while he simultaneously yelled polite suggestions to the lighting expert (everyone's old pal, Fred Kiriloff) and to the Polish choreographer, maintaining that Cocteau-type generous-octopus tact that made us each feel like the Only One. But there was not much to reminisce about, beyond what had become of his beautiful friend, George Reich, who had danced in our lamentable 1952 collaboration, the ballet *Dorian Gray*.

Because I regress with everyone to my age when first knowing them (with my parents, still acting the infant, with Paul Bowles the brash adolescent, with Lenny Bernstein the insecure goyische aspirer), now, before Jean Marais, I reverted to the intimidated starstruck expatriate.

A chain-smoking body builder, at fifty-six he's still beautiful in an old-fashioned Greek god manner, salt-&-pepper-colored hair with a forty dollar haircut. If not the official widow, he is at least the (unspoken) official heir to the Cocteau flair which now, at least in his custody, seems dry as a yellowing snapshot serving as the whole décor. For instance, our conversation was accompanied by the persistent replaying of Maurice Thiriet's score for a former production, music with no point of view toward either the present or the past, being a pastiche of the Honegger-Hollywood machines, yet which Marais feels disposed toward since Cocteau had once approved it. "Did Cocteau originally mean for the play to have music?" I asked. Marais answered, "Did Maeterlinck intend music for *Pélléas?*"

Thiriet then arrived, and Jean Marais introduced me as *"mon premier compositeur."* Together we followed the score filled with notes unrelated to those we were hearing, though no one including the composer appeared bothered. Suddenly Marais said—and I was very touched—"You're better now than you were then, maybe because, since I loved George, you were less visible."

Having time before my date with Pierre Bernac, I walked the length of Boulevard Montparnasse, pausing disturbed to let certain streets pass over me like perfume at an intermission, reactivating their molecules into the shape of vanished bookstores on the Rue Littré, or restaurants on the Rue de Vaugirard where every night of 1952 I dined with Henri Fourtine, or shadows near the Eglise Saint Roc where eighteen months earlier I was unfaithful to the future. Just as my return to Chicago ten years ago revolved around an involuntary search of façades behind which I had fallen in love as a child, so this afternoon, after leaving Jean Marais, the city echoed thunderously of my carnal twenties. For every bistro which excited the recall of a quarrel with Marie Laure or Julius Katchen, ten alleyways revived the swoon of furtive unions with sibling strangers whose white energy has now surely turned to gray decrepitude. A detour into the silent Rue Barbet de Jouy where, at number 16, very very high over the wall, some sycamore branches fluttered with vitality, but no other sign of life, in the street or house, nor any sound of music as when Marie-Blanche de Polignac was still alive.

All this, totally disengaged from my body now, had been nevertheless stamped irrevocably on Paris' heated streets through which I now was running, for night had fallen and I was *en retard*.

The sole thing in common between Pierre Bernac and Jean Marais is that both keep a great man's flame. Like our Frank O'Hara whose death gave birth to a flock of widows, Francis Poulenc is mourned by a proprietary clan of which Pierre Bernac is dean. Not that Pierre's interests are restricted—he teaches widely here and in America, the latter being a good deal more productive, he says—but to talk of his thirty years of concerts with Poulenc is to make his eyes shine like nothing else. We've spoken identically of this in other years, sipping the same tea in the same twilit room on the Motte-Piquet, sighing with pleasure at mutually favorite songs, with pain at mutually unfavorite singers. But now our leavetaking is sadder, because Pierre, about to be seventy, next month goes into the hospital.

At Robert Veyron-Lacroix', my little party is in full swing, champagne, orange juice, and Georgette Rostand. Nora takes me aside to announce that our lunch yesterday had proved exorcistic: last night she dreamed normally of Guy for the first time since he died. Lise Deharme, black empress from the insect kingdom on the arm of Jean Chalon, like everyone remarked on my dark hair, I having been blond during the fifties. Nobody wears maxicoats, and they all compare Boulez to Markevitch of forty years ago: creative genius turning to conducting sterility. At nine we watch the televised welcome of the astronauts.

To be dismayed by the astronauts' personal banality (are these the supermen we've spent milleniums developing!) is to mistake their robot role, their specialization as servants of separate higher minds. They deserve ticker tape as trained seals deserve dried fish.

A formal address from the Academy's Maurice Druon to these Americans was an eloquent, aphoristic, moving, well-built model of intelligence. The astronauts too, with earphones and grins, were a model of mannerly patience with their (to the French) childlike charm.

Long late *dîner en masse* with Nora, the Rostands, and Jacques Février plus his protégé, high in Montmartre at a new restaurant—recommended—called l'Assommoir. Although I first met Claude Rostand when he lectured in Fez with the Jeunesses Musicales in 1949 or 1950, we've talked only sporadically since. I was glad, therefore, to cement our acquaintance tonight, for I've always liked his mind which is that of a critic both cultured and articulate who owes these qualities, unlike American critics, to steady and long-lived personal intercourse with creative musicians of all persuasions. Attending warnings, he no longer smokes or drinks.

*

Thursday, 9 October

If there is one regrettable page in the *Paris Diary* it is about Nadia Boulanger. Not a word conforms with my true and gentler attitude toward that unusual woman. If possible, I would retract all. Still, apologies are somehow more undignified than insults. With Mademoiselle Boulanger silence is a wise tactic in matters extra-musical—if there are such matters: for her everything stems from or returns to music. To ignore that is to be the insolent falsifier who composed the diary pages.

With relief, therefore, I learned that Nadia Boulanger had invited me yesterday to visit, an invitation which, for geographical reasons, I was forced to decline. Today at noon, en route to Sauguet's, I left a gift with her concierge, and an envelope containing a few atoms of the respectful warmth of my feelings.

Despite the still heavenly weather, influenza's in the air, which dampened my appetite for Henri Sauguet's lunch of white melon, veal & mushrooms, salad, camembert, and red & blue grapes, served by his new and expert Tunisian cook. (Everyone—at least everyone I know—has lunch at home, prepared by a male servant from either Spain or North Africa.) New also is the blue-eyed cat, Parsifal, the replacement of the forty-pound angora who five years ago lunched with us, elegantly sitting among the dishware licking his haughty jaws, since perished in the jaws of a Bordelais fox.

Henri, forever the royalist, found Nixon's speech to the astronauts more moving than Druon's. Our conversation otherwise turned around the state of music, which we all know, except for our place in it. Henri at sixty-eight feels left behind, the wittiest man in France grows sad. The irony is reinforced when after lunch we visit his offices. These are in the nearby Rue Ballu, at the Société des Auteurs et Compositeurs Dramatiques, founded by Beaumarchais in 1777 and now under the absolute monarchy of Henri himself, whom all call Monsieur le Président. Placed in a sunny garden, the edifice is so stylish, like Druon's speech last night, so unrough, red leathered, and unofficial with a hothouse and birdcages; with Sauguet so kowtowed to, his sadness wears a halo.

Where now's the best pastry shop in our neighborhood? Chez Vaudron, à la Fourche, corner of the Avenues Clichy and Saint Ouen, used to sell us warm flaky orange custard tarts with real orange slices baked into them. Last week on discovering Vaudron's replaced by a hardware store, I was ready to take the first plane out of France. I would have, too, if a month ago I hadn't already made a date to dine tonight with Janet Flanner.

The idea of the meal was a strenuous expression of pleasure from Janet for my having turned nine portions of her "Letters from Paris," as they appeared in *The New Yorker*, into a piece for chorus and orchestra, at the Koussevitzky Foundation's behest in 1966. The published score had just appeared in a handsome edition, and I brought extra copies to Janet. "Nobody's ever done that to me before," she said, examining the musical notes printed above her dismantled text, as the taxi transported us from her hotel in Place Vendôme to a restaurant in Place des Victoires.

Three hours were passed over shrimp bisque, soles meunières, and a kilo of raspberries in thick cream, a long time considering we took no wine. Tonight as always Janet Flanner churned midwestern reticence into continental clarity. Circumspect in writing, she is outspoken in talk. As always she asked after my "dear Quaker parents," not failing to add, "What on earth did they feel about that pornographic diary?" And she examined me reproachfully through her monocle, resembling a hip and handsome Amazon disguised as George Washington playing Greek tragedy.

No one—certainly no one reviewing the Paris peace talks—reveals the French political scene to USA more lucidly than Janet Flanner (Genêt); she is as at home, articulate, and organized within this subject as she is within the visual arts. About current American writing she seems less informed, while her report on matters musical has dwindled to nothing. "My active musical knowledge ceased with a recognition of Debussy's whole tone scale, back in the teens of this century when I permanently quit the ugliness of Indiana for the beauty of this geography. I'd *like* to write about music, because God knows I have trouble sometimes finding material for the Paris letter. But I don't feel secure about it anymore, now that Doda Conrad and Noel Murphy aren't always around to go to concerts with. Am I missing much? It seems to me that France lacks all distinction since de Gaulle."

If she ignores the names of music critics here, she appears equally unconcerned with local society as Society, but adores gossip about the artistic rich. Her personal milieu, I gather, revolves more around the American expatriates of yore and of now, like Natalie Barney or Bettina Bergery or James Jones.

She hailed the waiter. I protested. "You can't pay, dear Janet. I'm a gentleman." "So am I," she answered.

As she had promised me a catalogue on Napoleon, I accompanied her to the Ritz where, since the demise of the Continentale last spring, she now inhabits a single room on the fifth floor overhanging the garden of the famous bar, with a treetop view of the obelisk on the left, and on the right the Eglise de l'Assomption's dome. It is a late October midnight, but a hyacinthine breeze enters the balcony window and ruffles for an instant the aquamarine nightgown which, earlier in the evening, a chambermaid had laid out on the narrow Spartan bed. "I'll probably die here," said Janet without passion, but with the straightforward poignance of one born in 1892.

The Ritz lobby contains a passageway one block long and two yards wide, bordered by mirrors and by several hundred display cases filled with luxury products representing the world's best stores. Empty and haunted now, at 1 A.M., I passed through it and onto the Rue Cambon where, in 1936, I spent a fortnight with my parents and sister Rosemary at the Hôtel de Castille which still stands there, unchanged.

*

Friday, 10 October

A bas Sartre, à bas Boulez, à bas Couperin, one hears the French kids cry. One doesn't hear American kids cry "Down with Goodman, down with Cage, down with Gottschalk," because they've never heard of these men, much less of Sartre, Boulez, or Couperin. Which is not to boast the superiority of French culture. The humblest French concierge knows the names, if not the works, of his country's cultural heroes for two thousand years, and is proud, while we, in a pinch, may know the names of Hemingway or Mailer (though not their works), but strictly as folk heroes.

They eat more sensibly than we, yet die young anyway.

They're all reading *Papillon*, the adventuresome memories of an escaped convict, or *Piaf*, the lubricious (and factually misinforming) memories of Edith's half-sister, or *Un peu de soleil dans l'eau froide* by Françoise Sagan who, second only to Doris Day, remains my inavowable female passion.

Lesser fixtures go, like the Vaudron pastry shop. And there's no more Madame Alice enthroned and immobile behind the zinc of the Reine Blanche. In fact, no more Reine Blanche. No more Arabs. Bigger numbers remain, but are washed clean of character. You now can buy wine in snap-open cans.

The biggest aspect of all—point of view—remains intact. Rightly or wrongly the French have always condescended to cultures beyond their frontiers. Before the New Wave of 1960 they admitted to no American influence, since what, after all, beyond our "barbarism," did we have to offer? Surely not so-called Serious Music. Except for Gershwin's, names like Copland or Harris or Sessions were merely names when I first arrived here, and are still merely names. The "barbarism" of jazz, which they respected (or rather were dazzled by), they quickly mistranslated into Ravel or Josephine Baker. Today they eagerly await *Easy Rider*, thrilled by America's freedom to do her own thing, ignoring that the freedom of the easy riders is no more self-questioning, no less assembly line, than the conformism of the fifty annual Miss America contestants.

Five P.M. This morning, spoke with Georges Auric who three hours earlier debarked from New York, of which his chief impression is that all the actors in *Oh! Calcutta!* are circumcised.

Shopping, rue de Rivoli. Mostly Lanvin and Rochas colognes. In Galliniani's the British edition of the *Paris Diary*, still at this late date, is prominently displayed. A clerk kept looking anxiously from me to my face on the book cover to me, but I didn't help him—how could I? Massive purchase chez Durand, the same as the purchases we used to make there: Chabrier, Messiaen, Satie, and, bizarrely, Schumann's *Pièces Fantaisistes*. A final visit to Didier Duclos, so that he could copy some tapes of *Lions* and *Sun*, in the heavy oaken offices of Boosey & Hawkes. Speaking with him of his predecessor, Mario Bois, proved only the Rashomonesque inutility of discussing the man with those who loved or loathed, or loved and loathed, him.

Back now for a nap before this evening's *sortie*.

*

Sunday midnight, 12 October

Less than two days remain. (. . . *Allons plus vit' nom de Dieu/Allons plus vit'* . . .) Friday, then, I picked up Jean-Michel Damase where—right next door

to my Alma Mater, the Ecole Normale—he lives with
his mother, harpist Micheline Kahn, to whom Ravel
granted the première of his *Introduction et Allegro*
in 1907. Since we would be supping after the ballet
(that gnawing hideous habit—the midnight supper),
Jean-Michel now offered me merely some thin cheese
sandwiches while he downed three fat whiskies, talking meantime (very man to conservative man) about
how "we" will survive *malgré tout*, how his new opera,
on a libretto excised by Louise de Vilmorin from her
Madame de, although only half completed, is scheduled
for Bordeaux next spring, and how Pierre Capdeveille
is dead. This talk transpired in a parlor indistinguishable from thousands of other ceiling-lit bourgeois
French parlors, except that it contained five harps. At
8:50 Jean-Michel introduced me to his beautiful mother, reading alone in her bedroom. Then he drove us in
his Citroën, like the still youthful spirit that he is, to
the Odéon in time for the 9 o'clock curtain just rising
on the execrable Lazzini ballets.

Joseph Lazzini, a second-rate Béjart (himself a
second-rate Petit, who is the poor man's Robbins), is
terribly up to date with his mixed media, and music
by none other than Mossolov—the *Iron Foundry*, at
that! The infinite relief of intermission brought rounds
of muscatel at the Méditéranée with Félix Labisse.
Saw Nouréev (as the French spell him) in the flesh,
and embraced dear Boris Kochno who seemed calm
and sober and more Old Russian than ever, and who
has just finished a deluxe book on Diagheleff who, like
Cocteau for Marais and Poulenc for Bernac, is the
joyful cross he'll bear till death.

Supper: in the now unrecognizable region of Les Halles at an unattractively lit actors' hangout with rubbery food and good wine, where Jean-Michel had a date who turned out to be an acrobat from the Folies Bergères, of weak intellect, strong beauty, and no little self-assurance. Bars until dawn.

Saturday very tired, still a queasy stomach and vaguely *enrhumé*. Party for me at the home of Nöel Lee, the favorite of us all, with guests comparatively young. When they all went home, Noël fixed an omelette. I got chills, and went home too.

Still exhausted this afternoon for the rehearsal with Gérard Souzay and Dalton Baldwin. Dalton, cheerful, served tea with cookies swiped from the Hungarian airplane that brought them yesterday from Budapest. Gérard, haunted, no longer just a dapper genius concerned with cultured swooners one recalls at Hélène Jourdan-Morhange's years ago, sounds marvelous, if insecure in English. My cycle, meant for him, indeed sounds meant for him. If they practice hard, and they will, the piece will work.

Went straight to Jeanne Ritcher's where Jacques Février and someone else sat around quibbling for two hours before we went, the four of us, to La Coupole— again those endless late meals. Their company, after the sober dedication of Souzay, seemed glib. Not that I am not superficial too, nor that the presumable courage of admitting the superficiality in any way eliminates it.

The Coupole was swarming and I was bored with

being pushed around, the slow service, and with my
friends' undignified ogling of the indeed hypnotically
handsome and enviable *jeunesse dorée*, so I quit them
midmeal and taxied across the city to my bed.

*

Monday, 13 October
Late afternoon

At the hour of executions an Italianate voice said,
"Ne quittez pas. Mademoiselle tient à vous parler.
We've been trying to reach you for days." Indeed,
I am seldom home. But Mademoiselle who? Then
Nadia Boulanger came onto the phone. "I wanted,"
she explained, "at least to hear your voice before you
left Europe, and to say adieu." Her own tremulous
voice, at once vivacious and ancient, belied her semi-
blindness at eighty-five, and her peculiar generosity
which can be defined only through itself, as in these
final words: *"Je veux quand même vous dire à bientôt.*
Evidemment ça ne veut rien dire, mais vous com-
prenez, pour moi ça doit tout dire." ["I'd like to say
I'll see you soon. That phrase obviously means nothing, but you understand, for me it must mean everything."]

Lunch at Marie Laure's, just the two of us. If,
between 1951 and 1957, we lunched in each other's
company about 300 times a year, and dined about 175
times a year, mostly in Paris and in Hyères; and if,
during the long summers of 1961 and 1964, we again
shared, in Hyères only, an additional 300 meals; then

today marks roughly the 3,220th time we've sat down to eat together, of which not more than 100 occasions were tête-à-tête, and fewer still in public and at my expense.

She was entranced with Boulanger's remark, a reaction proving once again—if proof were needed—that she, like Michel Girard, is "good" (there being no love lost between her and Nadia). On the other hand, mention of Julius and Denise gives rise to a screen of ennui merging with her Gauloise smoke, for she still kills three packs daily. Marie Laure hates death. Unlike Perquel, who constantly moons around the subject, she is intolerant even of her friends' sicknesses, and speaks of her own with sarcasm. Or used to. Despite pride in the horoscopic category of Scorpio, her sting is gone. (Born on Halloween, 1902, she claims an astrological link with myself, and the link's a mutual pact with the devil of eternal youth.)

Almost 100 percent self-involved, a childlike focus blurs her every borrowed opinion now, although her painting is more personal, clear, professional, and outgoing than ever. After lunch we spend an hour again inspecting her newest oils, certain of which I praise wholeheartedly, whereupon André is summoned to wrap one as a gift "for America." Another hour is passed thumbing through old scrapbooks: when finding a sudden photo of my former body, I'm stunned less by how the flesh decays (one learns early to blind oneself to that!), than by alterations in men's fashion. There we stood, Wilder Burnap, Boris Kochno, and me on the Saint Tropez jetty in April of 1951, trousers waving like granny skirts at our ankles, in contrast to crewcuts stoically braving the mistral.

Marie Laure escorts me to the great entrance hall where, beside the César sculpture, we say good-bye in the quotidian manner of our hello twelve days ago. This is the last time we will meet, since tomorrow I leave for London, then New York, and surely she will never return to America where her 1921 honeymoon provided "mixed impressions." Thus our casual kiss embodies an invisible farewell. Though I don't worry about her. As I leave (the wrapped picture neatly under my arm) a wild-haired young painter strewing autumn leaves passes me in the lobby, and goes immediately to embrace the Vicomtesse.

Henri-Louis de la Grange now lives three blocks from Place des Etats-Unis, a four-minute walk in the 5 o'clock sunshine. We passed a strained half-hour in his super-modern sky-high duplex. Strained, because twenty years ago Henri-Louis was a Fauré-playing Boulanger protégé who in turn protected the likes of Barber and Menotti while researching for a "definitive" biography of Mahler. After a series of transmutations, this honest and consecrated young man of means became, three years ago, a first-ranking promoter, financially as well as morally, of what the French call avant-garde (while remaining faithful to the still unfinished Mahler book). His current protégé is conductor-impresario Maurice Fleuret with whom he shares this luxury apartment as well as the woolen-eyed eagerness of sound and fury. Our common interests faded, Henri-Louis is nothing if not a gentleman while attempting to explain the "fact" of me to Fleuret who examined, briefly and without interest, my two burnt offerings—*Sun* and *Music & People*. (My cold grew worse, I began getting hives, phoned the Aurics to cancel our good-bye drink.) As we shook hands Henri-Louis thanked me for the information I'd mailed him thirteen years ago: about Mahler who, during an American visit in the early 1900's, met Charles Ives, and planned to program Ives' scores on forthcoming European tours. But Mahler's death annulled the project which might otherwise have changed the international face of music.

Tonight as prearranged Robert Kanters will take me to Moravia's comedy, symmetrically rounding out my visit with a little sleep.

*

New York City
October 23

In another time and place I may expand some impressions of the London week which was a climax rather than an anticlimax to the trip—assuming climaxes are feasible after forty when the predictability of even our most inventive friends begins to pall. At Moravia's play, for instance, I suffered investigatory stares from Christian Mégret, himself hardly the paragon he once was in Venice; later, chez Wepler in the Place Clichy where I invited Robert K. for a final supper, my once so valuable Jean Leuvrais joined us and cast the same cold eye. My French friends distressed me. The distress became translated into boredom: seeing myself in their eyes, their differentiation dissolved, which hurt, since it lay my infant ego bare. "When next I return," thought I, self-protectively, "you'll all be really old." That's unfair, if unimportant—they don't reason this way.

Still, you *can* go home again, and be welcomed warmly. If the experience proves sad, it's not that home has changed but that you have. To realize that seeing all these old acquaintances, one by one, or tightening professional contacts, or phoning critics and feeling the scene (as though musically it weren't the same everywhere, business, business, the business of pleasure)—to realize that it all equaled not one fresh tomato from the high heaps of tomatoes at the open market there, or the early evening lights on the Rue de la Jonquière, or the troubling black beauty of the midnight *pissotière* where anxiety-ridden heads float disembodied. Paris too floats disembodied, self-contained like a soap bubble, moving directionless, which I loved as a child and no longer need.

Still, my Paris is mine: firsthand reports of fact automatically diminish thirdhand fictions like, say, Frederick Brown's bio-abortion on Cocteau. Impersonally observed, the French capital appears in agony. Her present loveliness is of an autumn maple wearing the heavenly red of death, or of an old whore forced to the reality that cleanliness is next to godliness, yet who has not forgotten the art of applying eye shadow.

Today is my birthday, bringing me exhausted across

187

the homeland frontier where the customs inspector politely asks:

"You were abroad how long?"

"Twenty-one days."

"Value of your imported purchases?"

"Around fifteen dollars—of Rochas' Rose cologne for my mother."

"Was your trip for pleasure?"

"For pain."

14

Journal Two

LOVE is impossible. If it were possible, it wouldn't be love. To define romantic love is to miss the point. Such love can only be defined after the fact—yet how define what no longer exists? Lovers inhabit a cloud, free from space-time laws. The cloudburst signals an end to the honeymoon, a start to responsibility. Decades later they recall the cloudy life, but cannot refeel, and thus cannot specify, it. Memory of intensity becomes a vaguely embarrassing treasure.

Tristan and Isolde consumed a potion brewed to last three years, and died before the effect wore off. Like Romeo and Juliet, the appeal of their fame lies in their death. Had these "immortal" lovers survived, their affair would have evolved like all affairs: into accommodations broader than carnality. Romantic love belongs to youth, and is by nature too selfish, too isolated, to burn long without the nourishment of change. To an outsider, all young lovers are boring except those who are killed.

As to friendship—what the French call *camaraderie*,

or nonsexual love (if such a thing exists) —this differs from Romantic Love not in kind but in emphasis. Presumably it is less egoistic, more *caring*, and endures longer, similar interests and goals being as much involved as affection. (Lovers, while they last, need nothing in common beyond their bodies.)

None of this has changed since pre-history. Surely the New integration of colors and classes, flower people on a collision course, is old as the dictum that opposites attract. If their union creates explosion, that's another matter.

*

Our most neglected book is Jane Bowles' *Two Serious Ladies*, published a quarter century ago when the author was twenty-four. Although twice reprinted, with good reviews, the work has had minimal circulation. Its champions today are the same as yesterday, a staunch lunatic fringe for whom the book has become, so to speak, well known for being unknown. They find continuing vitality in the insane charm, the contagious invention, but also in the genetic influence of this novel. One trend of American fiction, in both style and matter (including much of McCullers, Williams, Capote, even Mrs. Bowles' husband Paul, and more recently Gavin Lambert, John Ashbery, and James Schuyler) would never have been quite the same without *Two Serious Ladies*.

Like Erik Satie's very special coterie music which is finally being enjoyed by a larger audience, perhaps Jane Bowles' only novel will one day be more widely read. I sincerely hope so—but I will regret it too. To share one's private discoveries with the public is a painful pleasure.

*

Esquire has just extended me a written invitation to pose nude in "a group photograph of notable people from many fields of endeavor." I phoned to ask who some of the "notables" would be and learned they were mostly Establishment types like Margaret Mead, Leonard Bernstein, Marshall McLuhan. I don't know how *they* reacted, or, indeed, if *Esquire* will manage to get its picture. But I wrote back as follows:

Through my musical composition and published prose I have already, like any artist worthy of the name, publicly stripped. I feel no further need to bare my literal flesh.

Total self-exposure communicably formalized: that's what the making of art is all about. This metaphor of life is convincing only when the artist undresses metaphorically, through his work. By definition his act reveals more than mere nudity, for the skin too is torn off, disclosing entrails and organs and blood with as many random colors as are found in rainbows and slaughterhouses. These colors are reassembled on canvas and stages, in words and melodies.

The process applies to all real creators as separate in space, time, and nature as Saint Augustine and Henry James, Phidias and Fragonard, even Bach and Boulez. (Admittedly the musical language is more "symbolic" than others: logicians cannot yet decipher a composer's secret and expose him, like Goya or Martha Graham, for indecent notions. The composer himself cannot tell you what he "means"; if he could, he would not compose.)

The process performed by those less talented amounts to a striptease wherein neither fallen veil nor resultant nakedness is put to further use. Unemployed, literal nudity signifies nothing but literal nudity. Nudity for its own sake becomes as embarrassing to the nude as to his public, for what could be more indicative that he is finally like everyone else? It is not demonstrable that the new permissiveness has been liberating, has rendered people less neurotic (as we used to say), or, above all, has *of itself* produced new works of cultural value among young radicals who confuse nudity with sexual frankness.

The new nudes imitate art, they aren't art. Art disguised as nudity is viable (Genet), but nudity disguised as art becomes at best a joke (Charlotte Moorman), at worst a bore (*Che!*).

If today artists still remain exposed through their work, what satisfaction do they further enjoy through self-exposure to the camera? Why, of course!—the satisfaction of publicity, publicity now being, as much as music, one of the lively arts. But if the quite legitimate art of, say, Andy Warhol lies essentially in being famous for his fame, he is at least not trying (as I would be) to have it both ways. Tempted though I also am, it would be ludicrous to disprove this point by disrobing (like the heartwrenchingly discombobulated father in *Teorema*) literally in public.

It goes without saying that I am against all censorship. Yet the current cashing in as an easy way out, the ever vaster imitations of the real thing, recalls Yeats's complaint that the coat he made with his song was caught by fools who wore it in the world's eyes. "Song, let them take it," he concludes, "for there's more enterprise in walking naked." Or, in the case today, there is more enterprise in walking clothed.

My position must therefore be symbolic if I pose for your picture. I will do so, provided I be the one fully-clad person in the group.

*

If publicity is an art, that art has evolved into crime. Andy Warhol was just shot with the casual violence his films illustrate: the unexpected as expected, and at its worst. Whatever the outcome, this may be the (very high priced) poetry of today. Robert Kennedy just died on television. Here I sit typing, a coward with the written word, wondering at the sky's turning today suddenly golden, which the weather report describes as Unseasonably Warm.

The New Art. Television cannot be of it. Art is reaction to, television is reporting of. TV's marvel springs from seeing the moment. That moment, frozen, reprojected tomorrow, cannot be reheated. Art stays warm. Art conceived for TV (*Amahl* presumably) works better on stage or on movie screens. Television by inherent definition is reportage. Reportage is not art, and when trying toward art (*In Cold Blood* presumably) it loses its built-in strength of spontaneity.

*

"Are any of my enemies here?" I ask my host, Norman Podhoretz, as he opens the door to Shirley and me at the grand assemblage which is his retort to Truman Capote's ball. He draws on his cigarette and answers proudly: "They're all your enemies."

*

Truman Capote, in adapting for other mediums his goodies of the past, gets a lot of mileage from a comparatively meagre output. His art has become his life. Like record dealers, he glories less in creation than in distribution. But distribution is *the* art of today. Nor will there be, in any case, posterity for anyone.

Andy Warhol's milieu contains no Negroes, for Negroes no longer just fool around. I look forward eagerly to all Warhol's new works. But I never go see them.

Edward Albee, when stating that *Mao, Box, Mao*'s characters are all really saying the same thing of course, leaves us no answer. The fact that he composed the play doesn't mean he "knows." They just aren't saying the same thing. Unless, according to how you slice it, we're all always saying the same thing: Stendhal and Aquinas, Aquinas and Charley Brown, Charley Brown and Ella Cinders, Ella Cinders and Stendhal: all discuss man's fate on some level. If the people in this "musical play" are indeed each saying the same thing, that thing is said at different speeds in different hues with different emphases. Different, as in the Lucia sextet, not similar as in a Bach fugue. For a spoken fugue can never succeed: it would be babel.

194

Tennessee Williams, obsessed with revision, forever returns to a basic material which he has now exhausted. No matter how long you polish a garnet, it never becomes a ruby.

*

> One must not confuse the poetry of revolution with a revolution in poetry. A revolution in poetry can only occur in a country free from internal wars.
> —COCTEAU, *Lettre à Maritain* (1925)

An artist may see deeper than others, but only into himself. Even then, his explanations are superfluous and suspect. Never ask his advice about a neighboring art. How can he know about that? Never listen to him on politics. Don't listen to me.

Much dance today seems less deranged than the music that supposedly impels it. Music and dance may swing hand in hand but never marry, for if music does impel dance, does dance impel music? And the only painting that ever had political influence was of Uncle Sam soliciting our boys into the service: I WANT YOU.

Can a land in revolt produce art other than the revolt itself? If, as remarked at the end of "The Avant-Garde as Démodé," art reflects the environment, then renders it bearable, the rendering is not through sugar-coating but through objectification. No matter how conventional or experimental the artist's language, his voice will be heard as timely without his consciously trying. The fashionable slogan "Medium as Message" cannot be translated by "Art as Politics." Art *does* reflect politics, but cannot *be* politics any more than oil can be water.

Politics and art run parallel but at different tempos, sometimes merging at the crossroads of propaganda, as in Stalinist Russia or in America today.

Sooner or later the *arrière-garde* comes up and bangs the *avant*. The New, when you scrape off topsoil, is as traditional as good manners used to be. And any work of art that lasts is built with discipline. Art that lasts is not a consideration of the pop generation. Discipline and manners are for the moment not even memories but they will be rediscovered and ironically form the basics of another aristocracy which in turn will be called avant-garde.

*

The artist is like everyone else, only more so. His feelings are not necessarily deeper than other people's, but he communicates them with a formality that goes beyond space and death, touching human hearts in a special way. Just how these hearts are touched is an inherently nineteenth-century question, one not asked by classical artisans like Bach, nor by many today when the concept of artist-as-individual is dissolving.

Today is nothing if not scientific. Thus it is intriguing, in Stanley Burnshaw's new book, to find the Romantic query reopened as a biological investigation. The gradual enmeshing of fact with novel fact, image

upon strange image, weaves a web which welcomes
us despite ourself.

Burnshaw declares: "Poe had fooled a generation
of more than receptive French writers with his fanciful
account of the writing of 'The Raven' [in *The Philosophy of Composition*] only to reverse himself later:
'With me poetry has not been a purpose but a passion, etc.' "

Why "fanciful"? Does the fact that Poe scrupu-
lously plotted "The Raven" prevent it from being a
passion? Form and order do not spring from fancy,
yet they are urgent to a self-contained poem. Ravel
maintained that *The Philosophy of Composition* had
influenced him more than any piece of music; using
it as a model, Ravel produced some of our century's
most "inspired" sounds.

And when Burnshaw quotes Mozart, "My ideas
come as they will, I don't know how," I feel certain
Mozart didn't care how, either.

The author continues: ". . . I have heard of few
well-known works other than Henri Michaux's poems
and drawings which were actually created while drugs
were controlling the mind." Which few? A dimension
is lacking here. Yes, an artist may be born chemically
different with his built-in mescaline, just as the mesca-
line-taker will come to have built-in perceptions. But
these perceptions will never make of the mescaline-
taker an artist. The author foresees this objection,
since he leaves no stone unturned to discover *who*
the artist is. How will he find out, until he admits the
possibility that the artist is just like anyone—but
no one is like the artist? *Who* does the writing? That

question, which interests artists less than scientists, was not even posed before the eighteenth century. It's a Romantic query, presupposing the artist to be special. Being inside looking out, an artist doesn't ask the question any more than a child asks how he learned to speak (much less to explain how language works, which nobody's ever done). Geniuses do not hold genius in awe, nor even think in terms of genius, at least not of their own—except for what it can get them.

*

Talent, like personality, results from a combination of accidents. Virtually all artists feel that their talents give their personality carte blanche, and virtually all artists are wrong. But what can they do: they must protect their accidents with the Romantic holdover. In the classical era there were no such accidents; then again, there were no such artists, they were craftsmen.

Today are we returning to craftsmanship, or at least an *idea* of it, and a craftsmanship predating Classicism? Yes, to collective workers, a mass of apprentices without a master. Yet every one of these apprentices has the put-upon ego of a nineteenth-century genius, and a keen sense of twentieth-century gold.

On page 28 of *Forbidden Colors* Yukio Mishima announces: "In this world it is believed art and reality live quietly side by side; but art must dare to break the laws of reality. Why? In order that it alone may exist." For many of the young the laws of reality have already seemingly been broken: for them art alone exists. But if only art exists, by the same token, no art exists.

On page 25 of the December 12, 1969, issue, *Time* magazine asserts: "[The hippie movement] has drawn all sorts of people: the rebellious, the lonely, the poets, the disaffected, and worse." No comment. Except *The Poets and Worse* makes a great title.

*

The live artist's output is an animate perspective. An obituary is a static retrospective.

My obituary will be my work. That work is now in a constant flow of becoming. How can I pause to objectify the motion? Obituaries look over the shoulder. What could I tell about the music that the music doesn't tell? To chisel the notes onto a marble slab would be merely redundant. An artist able to assess his own work is already dead.

*

I do not "believe" in ghosts, poltergeists, contacting of the so-called spirit world, or divination of a universal order, since examples of these inevitably have a logical, rather than mystical, explanation. I do believe in ESP, but have seen it to be effective only in the uneducated—those unhampered by intellectual barriers. Palmistry and astrology apparently contain some truth, but the comparative results of specialists are too contradictory to be useful. Yoga is good for the body. Scientology I'm told is a destructive sham. The *I Ching* appeals to one type of person whose enjoyment of the Orient is surface and quick. As to clairvoyance, I do not credit it at all: the future cannot be read for it does not exist; if the future existed it would not, by definition, be the future. Certain religious systems over the milleniums have obviously proved workable. I myself was raised a Quaker, and would have remained an active practitioner were I not also a composer. You will find that most artists aren't much concerned with mysticism or extra-sensory perception as subjects of conversation. The meaning, whatever it is, of such things is concentrated within art forms: its discussion seems relevant only to laymen.

*

The trouble with gurus, they are so noisy in their meditation.

*

Seymour Krim's article in *Playboy* is pleasant and revealing, but its major proposition is unsound. Pleasant, because it comes as antidote to his abject obsession with Norman Mailer recently printed in *New York* magazine. Revealing, because it pictures him still flirting with the role of novelist he never became. (The entire article is redolent of long-winded 1930's saga-prose known as ballsy.) The unsound proposition—that the novel is dead, and that self-revelatory formats are supplanting it—preoccupies this note.

During the fifties the novel was merely dormant, criticism of criticism of the novel (not to mention reportage as high art) having momentarily displaced it as *the* literary outlet, especially here and in France (though not in Japan where the novel bloomed pure). During the sixties the French novel reawakened vengefully through Claude Simon, Alain Robbe-Grillet, Jean Cau, Claude Mauriac, Michel Butor, to name but five. Their experiments in turn stimulated America's more interesting fictionalists like Harry Mathews, James Salter, James Merrill, Hortense Calisher, Susan Sontag, while the good old novel-as-narrative continues through the staying power of Vladimir Nabokov, or through monumental Jews such as Bellow, Malamud, Gold, or through the revitalization of such as James Purdy, Joyce Carol Oates, or Alfred Chester whose stories are nothing if not, as we now say, relevant.

To say there is no fixed form for Novel, is to underline the obvious. A novel is a novel if its author says so. The novels of Defoe, Austen, Conrad, Dos Passos, and Djuna Barnes hardly resemble each other, though all are surely autobiographical. (Similarly in music. Although Sonata has a dictionary definition, Beethoven, who wrote thirty-two piano sonatas, found thirty-two ways of changing the definition.)

Krim nevertheless lists those whom he feels fall into the category of "ex-novelist, the new communicator we can already see in the early and various stages of his making." The list, on which to my bemusement I find myself, is unconnected to his premise that today's author can no longer afford to hide behind the "mask of fiction" but must commit himself to "total communication" by his "driving need for direct participation in our national life." Certainly the "new" speech of the writers mentioned would go unheeded but for the already established renown of those writers. If Norman

Podhoretz were not a famous editor why would we care about his making it? Were Taylor Mead not a superstar who would glance at his diary? If Mailer weren't Mailer would we buy his history of the Pentagon march (which he labels Novel, and relates in the third person)? Certainly my *Paris Diary* was accepted largely on the strength of whatever notoriety I may have had as a composer; and certainly I am not an ex-novelist, nor do I feel a driving need to participate. Diaries are a sideline, notebooks wherein an artist records his problems of work and play. Nearly always, though, they are kept with the intention of being read; so like all art they dissimulate by becoming a sort of code. The diarist doesn't present himself but an idea of himself, and only that idea of himself which he chooses to publicize.

As a literary form the diary is hardly new (indeed, it is far older than the novel), except as an indigenous American utterance, public confession not having been our bent until recently. Confession is the distinguishing ingredient of diaries. Yet confession risks adopting the features of the very mask that Krim says novelists hide behind. Our century's best known diarist, André Gide, during the blitzes of World War II blissfully notated adventures with Arab boys in his Biskra retreat. To tell it like it is, is no more a property of diaries than of fiction. Lives are not facts, nor does the present moment exist; an author can necessarily record the present only after the fact.

How, asks Krim, can we suffer from too much truth? Of itself truth is not persuasive, even less is it art. And who, including the diarist himself, can prove that the character represented is, in this guise, finally, the *real* author? Does Baudelaire's journal disclose more to us of Baudelaire than Genet's novels do of Genet? Could Philip Roth actually have composed that recent complaint in another form without its becoming more rather than less of a mask? To fictionalize the real can make it easier for an author to be honest. The realist novel of the thirties has become the unrealistic autobiography of the sixties.

Seymour Krim's wistful plea for the reinforcement of sincerity through new forms is understandable. Still, all real works of art (be they geometric sculptures, children's poetry, or reports on Hanoi) speak to us, by definition, with their creator's voice.

The 1960's are nearly gone as we look back and compare. John Gruen has come to interview me about the fifties. The fifties! But I said it all in the diaries which cover exactly that decade. Or did I? Diaries and memoirs are diametral. What I might tell now about that era becomes conscious recall, while a diary is history *qui s'ignore.* We are, John and I, history which is not yet but will become, as we sit in this room drinking our pale sauterne and steaming coffee. The pale steam evaporates almost instantly. The time we waste—our daily toiletries—eventuate into nostalgia. Still, nostalgia is useful waste. Someday we will recall these minutes of discussion about recalling minutes of discussion. Are the fifties, those used-up years, already history about which nothing can be done except reminisce for John? They were a time for individuals as opposed to our blurred collectivity, for I love you—rather than Love. We each have our decade of deciding who we are, then a decade of proving to others we are who we decided. We are history without knowing it. A diary is not nostalgia (though it may write of the past) because it defines Now, a Now which can be reread years from now. Your heyday decade is usually the post-high-school one, the period you physically recapture in your dotage. At eighty-five, crew-cutted and saddle-shoed, I'll strut the Big Apple.

Am I a sixties' writer, a sixties' composer? No, because my work does not show me to be *engagé*. Does it? Never have so many first-rate artists been so politically involved, yet will commitment of itself make them first rate rather than merely (merely!) responsible citizens? I represent the times if for no other reason than that I inhabit them. Last spring the *Times* asked a number of writers if during the coming summer they planned to be *involved*. They all seemed to be filling out their own report card as though some cultural Big Brother were looking over their shoulder.

*

This book will be called *Critical Affairs* since that's what it mainly is. Indeed, many of the pieces seem critical not only in the sense of being appraisals, but of being concerned with "critical" turning points or crises, and also of being plain captious, even hypercritical.

One-half of the ingredients are outright complaint. Take "Against Rock." I do not say that people need be responsible, even to each other, although in a way

I believe they should: certainly interhuman responsibility holds a key to the "difficult" meaning of much art today (such as Buñel's or Antonioni's). I do say that once one accepts a responsible job, like music criticism, the job should be practiced responsibly. I am not against rock, only against the pretentious claims of rock criticism. In a broader sense I tried to convey this in "Critics Criticized." But if complaint is easier than praise, it is also more important (at least in contemporary non-fiction) because more urgent. We complain about what concerns us—usually about mediocrity in high places; since mediocrity is nearly everywhere the rule, not to say the danger, to complain is necessary. To praise is a luxury, for the praiseworthy does not *concern* us, at least not in the same way. In itself praise seldom makes literature, unless what is being praised becomes illuminated as praiseworthy *for the first time.* Even then, we usually find a complaint lodged in the heart of the matter. For instance, when Brigid Brophy reveals Françoise Sagan as a genuine artist (the way Stravinsky once revealed Tchaikovsky), Miss Brophy is putting us down (we should have known about Sagan all along!) and thus criticizing us more than praising her subject. . . . If constructive laments on the state of the world as well as on the state of letters now attain that self-nourishing lucidity once identified as art, non-literary expressions in attempting similar clarity succeed less well. Protest through music is not so convincing as words about protest through music. Now words about protest through music, inasmuch as they do convince, are insolent and ultimately decadent. For they are not the real thing. And the real thing, as I said at the start of this book, is having a bad time today. So as a composer-writer I place myself simultaneously in frying pan and fire.

The other half of the ingredients are cheerfuller, if looser. Hence the alternate name, *A Composer's Journal*. Of the through-written essays, "Décors of Sound" first appeared with the subtitle, "From the Diary of Ned Rorem"—an excuse for the ungainly sequence of paragraphs linking music to interior decoration, a subject far from my heart. Elsewhere the book is literally a diary, the verbal mode in which I feel most at home, not because, as Krim contends, it speaks "truth," but because it legitimatizes radical shifts in feeling: the free-flowing aphoristic tone provides an antidote to the discipline imposed on my music. . . . *Vogue* asked for something "geared toward youth," because inherently youth is always news, and news, alas, today is always right—though only while it remains news, that is, for a split second. So "The Avant-Garde as Démodé" is already démodé, the Living Theatre and other friends having quickly become mere recollections, and blurred ones at that, like pain which is harder than pleasure to duplicate in memory. . . . Rock no longer even bores me, it doesn't exist. This is not condescension; I am just more occupied otherwise. (I do deplore Colin Davis' quip: rock is like pimples that disappear after adolescence. A gentler analogy would be: rock resembles puppy love which can paradoxically last a lifetime because it introduces the heart to vulnerability, an emotion which, if suppressed, makes living only half living.)

The dangers of datedness have been risked by every author since Petronius who has dealt with the quotidian, but especially today in art which so rapidly turns into history. That's why certain authors have made of the risk a virtue, why datedness itself becomes subject matter, and why some readers are charmed every New Year's Day to find, in the rotogravure section, purportedly objective surveys of the previous twelve months, months of which the readers are now commodiously rid.

Datedness also furnishes the life blood of a daily journal. "Twenty Years After," though, recounts a two-week return to Paris not yet quite outmoded enough to provide the mellowness of distance, yet already too far past to project current dimensions. Its author is no longer myself.

This morning a cablegram brought me the news of Marie Laure's death. From the intelligent warmth of her friendship I learned more than I ever learned from anyone, or from any one experience like LSD or a love affair. Without her, an epoch is closed for a whole society, the world's weight's altered. For fifteen years she was France to me. How can my recent report sound other than frivolous now, when I am inhabited by that nausea of loss which renders futile the ambitious gesture of publishing a book?

INDEX